Experiencing Mystagogy: The Sacred Pause of Easter

Gerard F. Baumbach

Paulist Press

New York/Mahwah, New Jersey

The Publisher gratefully acknowledges use of the following: Scripture selections are taken from the New American Bible Copyright © 1991, 1986, 1970 by the Confraternity of Christian Doctrine, 3211 Fourth St., N.E., Washington, D.C. 20017-1194 and are used by license of the copyright owner. All rights reserved. No part of the New American Bible may be reproduced in any form without permission in writing from the copyright owner. Excerpts from the English translation of the *Catechism of the Catholic Church* for the United States of America © 1994, United States Catholic Conference, Inc.–Libreria Editrice Vaticana. Used with permission. Excerpts from the English translation of *The Roman Missal* © 1973, International Committee on English in the Liturgy, Inc. (ICEL); excerpts from the English translation of *Rite of Christian Initiation of Adults* © 1985, ICEL. All rights reserved. Excerpts from *The Works of Saint Cyril of Jerusalem*, Vol. 2, translated by L. P. McCauley and A. A. Stephenson (Fathers of the Church, Vol. 64), copyright 1970, The Catholic University of America Press; excerpts from *St. Ambrose: Theological and Dogmatic Works*, translated by R. J. Deferrari (Fathers of the Church, Vol. 44), copyright 1963, The Catholic University of America Press. Used with permission. Excerpts from *Commentary of Theodore of Mopsuestia on the Lord's Prayer and on the Sacraments of Baptism and the Eucharist*, Woodbrooke Studies, Vol. 6, edited and translated by A. Mingana, copyright 1933 by W. Heffer & Sons Limited, Cambridge, England. Used with permission. Excerpts from *St. John Chrysostom: Baptismal Instructions*, translated and annotated by P. W. Harkins (Ancient Christian Writers, Vol. 31), published by Newman Press, New York, copyright 1963 by Rev. Johannes Quasten and Rev. Walter J. Burghardt, S.J. Reprinted by permission of Paulist Press, Mahwah, NJ. Excerpt from editorial ("Give Them Something To Eat") by Stephen T. De Mott, M.M. from July/August 1994 issue (p. 7) of *Maryknoll* Magazine. Used with permission. Lines from "Song of the Open Road" from *Leaves of Grass* by Walt Whitman in Mark van Doren, *Walt Whitman: The Viking Portable Library* (New York: The Viking Press, 1945 [revised in 1973 by Malcolm Cowley]), 166-167. The poems "Water" and "He Was" by Thomas E. Durkish, Brant Lake, NY. Used with permission. The poem "Baptism" by Elaine Holena-Baumbach, 1978. Used with permission.

Photo credits:
p. 18, NASA; p. 19, Mia et Claus; p. 53, T. E. Durkish; p. 54, G. Baumbach; p. 68, Mia et Claus; p. 93, G. Baumbach; p. 115 top, G. Baumbach; p. 115 collage top, G. Baumbach; p. 115 collage middle, Mia et Claus; p. 115 collage bottom, G. Baumbach; p. 116, G. Baumbach; p. 156, T. E. Durkish; p. 171, G. Baumbach; p. 199, Gene Plaisted; p. 238, G. Baumbach; p. 242, G. Baumbach.

Cover design and illustration by James F. Brisson.

Nihil Obstat: Sr. Sheila Browne, R.S.M.
Censor librorum
September 6th, 1995

Imprimatur: Most Reverend John R. McGann, D.D.
Bishop of Rockville Centre
November 7th, 1995

Baumbach, Gerard F.
Experiencing mystagogy : the sacred pause of Easter / by Gerard F. Baumbach.
p. cm.
Includes bibliographical references.
ISBN 0-8091-3615-5 (alk. paper)
1. Mystagogy—Catholic Church. 2. Spiritual formation—Catholic Church. 3. Catholic Church—Prayer-books and devotions—English. 4. Eastertide—Meditations. I. Title.
BX2045.I55B38 1995
248.4'82—dc20 95-31453
CIP

Published by Paulist Press
997 Macarthur Boulevard
Mahwah, New Jersey 07430

Printed and bound in the United States of America

Contents

Preface	xi
Introduction	1
Chapter 1: The Challenge of Your Life of Faith	17
Chapter 2: Your New Life of Faith	49
Chapter 3: The Center of Your Life of Faith	81
Chapter 4: The Fullness of Your Life of Faith	113
Chapter 5: The Way, Truth, and Life of Faith	146
Chapter 6: The Spirit of Your Life of Faith	179
Chapter 7: Your Mission for Your Life of Faith	213
Epilogue	249
Notes	251

Dedication

To

Elaine

my wife

companion

friend

and to

Jason

Matt

and

Dan

who have given and loved

Acknowledgments

Many people played important roles in helping to bring this project to fruition and to completion, and I am especially grateful to them.

Special thanks are due Lisa, Bob, and Bonnie, parish neophyte readers at Saint Sylvester's Parish in Medford, New York. This wonderful group of three faith companions used this book in its original form to aid their reflection on their experience of initiation into the Church. The citations attributed to newly baptized persons that appear in this book are from these kind and wonderful people.

I also wish to acknowledge with special thanks Tom and Sue, parish catechumenate team leaders at Saint Sylvester's Parish when this project was first conceived, for their assistance in coordinating this project and in participating in the review process. Saint Sylvester's Parish was a model of initiation ministry to me; the banners that are recreated in chapter 5 reflect the phrases from banners that hung in Saint Sylvester's Church during the catechumenal journey.

Part of my formation in catechumenal ministries came during the introduction of the *Rite of Christian Initiation of Adults* at my own parish, the Church of the Curé of Ars, in Merrick, New York. To all who were part of these beginning years—pastoral staff, team members, catechumens, candidates, neophytes, and parishioners—I thank you for sharing with me our parish's faith journey into the richness of the rites and experience of initiation.

I also cite with great joy the creative and insightful efforts of Reverend Charles W. Gusmer, S.T.D., Reverend

Donald Hanson, and Dr. Brennan Hill, all of whom read and evaluated the book's chapters in their original form. Their suggestions and insights were particularly helpful in shaping and finalizing the original version. Father Gusmer also graciously agreed to offer additional review of the final work published by Paulist Press. To these three readers and to all of the parish participants, I offer timeless thanks and heartfelt admiration for their support of a dream come true.

Sister Catherine Dooley, O.P., Ph.D. has been a friend and supporter of my mystagogical meanderings for many years. I am indebted to her not only for her review of the final work, but also for her willingness to write the preface for the book. I am honored by Kate's participation in this project in this way and am buoyed by her support of my efforts on behalf of Christian initiation ministries.

Dr. Norman F. Josaitis, friend and colleague, kindly and gently shared his keen insights and helpful nuances during the preparation of the present work. His ability to adjust a phrase and evoke richer meanings to the matter at hand helped to make the final work even more precise in its presentation. For this assistance, I am truly grateful.

The enthusiastic guidance and support of three other persons, all professors at New York University when this idea was conceived, also must be happily acknowledged. To these friends—Dr. Margot Ely, Dr. Norma Thompson, and Dr. Gabriel Moran—I express my deepest gratitude, respect, and admiration for their extraordinary ways of moving me to probe, to investigate further, to see beyond the obvious. Margot Ely is a woman of boundless energy who engaged me in a project search that often led to self-exploration and new discoveries. Norma Thompson, a model of Christian discipleship, gently reminded me of the wonder of things religious and of layers of meaning in all of life's events. Gabriel Moran, mentor and friend, invited me into a conversation that lasted several years—on Saturday mornings, weekday evenings, at office meetings, group gatherings (often around a meal)—and that empowered me to look deep within myself for what he had already glimpsed. I am and remain indebted to Gabriel for his support and friendship, and for being "my teacher."

Finally, I am privileged to have worked with Maria L. Maggi, editor for Paulist Press. This thoroughly professional and highly skilled editor knew the manuscript "inside-out" and maintained extraordinary attention to every detail of the project. I have learned much from her about the industry in which we both serve, and I am proud to call her friend. To her and to all of her colleagues at Paulist Press, I extend my deepest appreciation.

The manuscript was word processed in its final version by Feng Chen, whose attention to deadlines was a welcome relief as the book moved toward completion.

All of the support of colleagues and friends in catechumenal, catechetical, and liturgical ministries notwithstanding, the responsibility for what is presented here remains solely my own.

Preface

The *Rite of Christian Initiation of Adults* is one of the most significant results of liturgical renewal. Over the past twenty years catechumens have been initiated and faithful have been renewed through the rites that center on conversion and faith. The implementation of this rite has brought about the restoration of the interrelationship between catechesis and liturgy and an explicit effort to take liturgical catechesis seriously. The *Catechism of the Catholic Church* notes that the liturgy is "the privileged place for catechizing the People of God" (1074) and that the aim of liturgical catechesis is "to initiate people into the mystery of Christ (It is 'mystagogy.') by proceeding from the visible to the invisible, from the sign to the thing signified, from the 'sacraments' to the 'mysteries'" (1075).

The *RCIA* has outlined the components of a liturgical catechesis in broad strokes, describing mystagogy as the time in which the community and the neophytes deepen and appropriate their comprehension of the paschal mystery through reflecting on the gospel, celebrating the Eucharist and hastening to do good works.

In the fourth and fifth centuries of the Church's tradition, the term mystagogy designated the post-baptismal catechesis that inspired the newly baptized to think back on the readings and the rites experienced on "that most holy night." During Easter week the bishop, in the midst of the gathered community, probed the images and narratives of the rite so that in reflection on the experience might come insight. The purpose of the bishop's homily was not to explain but to help the newly baptized enter into a sacramental vision of life in order to be transformed. Gerard Baumbach in *Experiencing Mystagogy: The Sacred Pause of Easter* has made a significant contribution to a contemporary mystagogy, in being one of the first authors to put theory into practice. Written for neophytes and their communities, he transposes the process of the ancient catechumenate to new situations and events and develops an integral paschal theology. The book is written in such a way that it calls forth participants rather than just readers. Each chapter in the book provides a means of reflection on each of the Sundays of the Easter season and challenges the newly baptized to live the paschal mystery of Christ. The neophytes are encouraged, however, to look upon "mystagogy as not just fifty days of the season, ending on Pentecost, but the time that follows as well." The newly baptized are reminded that each time the Church gathers for worship it is participating here and now in the mystery of faith: Christ has died, Christ is risen, Christ will come again.

The model that Dr. Baumbach proposes is designed for the Sundays of Easter but can be used for any Sunday throughout the year. Each of the reflections centers on a sacramental image and explores the relationship of that image to life experience, to the scriptures and liturgy, and calls for a personal response to the challenge of faith. The paschal mystery as it is celebrated weekly by the assembly in the eucharistic liturgy and as it is lived out in everyday works of justice and reconciliation is at the heart of each of these reflections. The paschal mystery is not an abstraction but the paradigm of the Christian life. The author includes some of the homilies of the fourth century bishop-teachers to illustrate that the death, resurrection and glorification of Christ can only be understood in the context of the whole history of salvation. The rhetoric of the early bishops about the paschal character of salvation is punctuated with biblical images of creation and destruction, freedom and slavery, death and life, Red Sea and desert, covenant and memorial. In the reflections on the images of the homilies, Dr. Baumbach leads the reader/participants to an awareness of the depth of the covenant relationship and to understand that Christ is present in the Church's sacramental celebrations by the action of Christ and the power of the Holy Spirit.

Two other themes are woven through each of the chapters. *Experiencing Mystagogy* promotes a sacramental vision that forms the context for the celebration of the sacraments. The sessions enable the reader/participants to "get beneath the symbols of the liturgy of initiation," to interpret them in the light of faith, and to become aware that it is grace that underlies that experience. The second theme is Catholic identity. A sacramental celebration is woven from signs and symbols that hold out a shared vision. This vision gives the community as a whole and those who constitute it a sense of belonging and a sense of direction. The author encourages the neophytes to nurture relationships with others as a people shaped and formed by the scriptures, as a eucharistic people, a discipleship people in a society that needs the Christian vision.

Gerard Baumbach describes the mystagogue as a catechist for the Easter season who is a wisdom seeker and a resurrection thinker. Indeed, in *Experiencing Mystagogy: The Sacred Pause of Easter*, he is that mystagogue for all who read this book.

Catherine Dooley, O.P.
Associate Professor of Religion and Religious Education
Catholic University of America

Introduction

From the baptismal waters and first sharing at the table of the eucharist emerge a "walk in newness of life" (*RCIA,* #244).[1] As a newly baptized person, or neophyte, you are accompanied by other believers on the eucharistic path of assembly prayer, parish identity, mutual support, and ongoing formation. Now that you have passed through the waters of new birth, you are invited to discern the meaning of the mysteries for your evolving story of discipleship in Jesus Christ. You have entered into the water—doused or immersed or dampened or soaked—and have celebrated with the faith community at the table of the Lord.

Some water experiences are indeed memorable—for example, surviving a flood, struggling to aim a fire hose at a burning inferno, bathing one's baby for the first time. Some also may be endings and beginnings all blended together; one may look back on all that led up to a key experience and then look beyond it to the future. Perhaps such an experience could be described as a sacred pause—when time stands still yet simultaneously moves so slowly and swiftly.

You may never actually "dry off" from your baptism. The Church did not quickly "towel-dry" you to restore you to a former self or, worse, to prepare you for casting as from a preformed baptismal mold. Just as ocean waves that flow randomly or lake breezes that redirect a lake's waters reshape the sands of a shoreline, so, too, does your parish continue to share in shaping who you are as a disciple of Jesus and member of the Church. The mold for this shaping is your experience of initiation into the Church and ongoing sharing in the eucharist; the craftspeople are the Spirit-filled community of believers who celebrate eucharist with you and continue to care for and about you.

Your Sacred Pause

Your experience of initiation into the life of the Church, the word of God in the scriptures, and the sacraments of initiation—baptism, confirmation, and eucharist—are the focus of this book. The book is written to support you in replaying, retelling, and recounting your experience of sharing sacramentally with your parish in the paschal mystery—that mystery of Christ's passion, death, and resurrection. This book invites you to pause now as you explore what your discipleship in Jesus Christ is becoming for you. Along the way of becoming is a need to pause periodically to reassess not only where you are but who you are. As you become, you pause not alone, but with your parish community of faith, for your story of who you are and what you are becoming is part of the story of the Church.

Experiencing Mystagogy: The Sacred Pause of Easter is intended to help you weave together some of your experiences and images of your conversion to Christ and initiation into the Christian faith. The book provides you with the opportunity to walk in the newness of life by:

- uncovering your experience of water-font and eucharistic table, of symbol and sacrament;
- exploring initiation into the community of believers, especially through the events of the vigil of Easter;
- becoming a partner in the life of your parish;
- discovering how you are changed by word and sacrament, offered with and by this community of disciples who walk with you;
- exploring what death and resurrection are now for you, in light of your parish's weekly celebration of the eucharist.

Why call this book an aid to your experience of mystagogy? Why use such an unusual term? The *Rite of Christian Initiation of Adults*, the framework for incorporating people into the Christian faith, describes mystagogy as "a time for the community and the neophytes together to grow in deepening their grasp of the paschal mystery and in making it part of their lives through meditation on the Gospel, sharing in the eucharist, and doing the works of charity" (*RCIA*, #244).[2] From hearing the proclamation of the gospel and through reflecting on your experience of the sacraments of initiation, you can come to a heightened sense of what conversion to Christ is for you and your parish.

As you reflect on your experience of initiation, you may see things differently. You may have a renewed discovery of the grace-filled life with God as seen through your relationships with family, friends, and parish. You may come to a new awareness of the Church, of the way the Church worships, lives, and serves. You may find new meanings in what it is for Christians to live in your community, your state, or the world. You may find new challenges to your faith and seek the wisdom to deal with such challenges creatively from deep within your heart. All of this occurs as your story unfolds on the walk in the newness of life, journeying now to Pentecost and beyond, for you are part of the story-formed journey of the Church.

Exploring Mystagogy

Mystagogy is neither a summary of what you did as a catechumen nor a retelling of what you may have learned already about the Christian faith. Mystagogy is also not a time for trying to "make room" for all that was not discussed or presented prior to baptism. Nor can mystagogy be compared completely or adequately to a "let-down time" similar to what sometimes happens after a graduation.

The experience of the Easter Vigil that shapes the mystagogical period is an opening to new life, not a conclusion resulting in separation from one's co-travelers. For example, the long baptismal robe is not an academic gown like the kind worn at commencement ceremonies. Rather, it is a signal to all to maintain the new status of the neophyte: to be clothed with Christ always, to walk *together* in the newness of life and not away from the gift and table of life.

Mystagogy is that catechesis after baptism that enables you to explore what death and resurrection are now for you, renewed each Sunday in the Church's eucharistic celebration. The liturgy of the Easter events unfolds during the period of mystagogy, always to be reviewed and renewed in light of your own story of coming to faith in Jesus Christ.

The ongoing support of your parish, your "spiritual womb" all during the catechumenate, remains an essential need after baptism as well. In addition to sponsors, godparent(s), parish catechumenate team, and parish priest(s), your partner in this journey is the "mystagogue," a catechist for the Easter season who is a wisdom-seeker, a resurrection-thinker who sees victory in the death and raising to new life of Jesus. The mystagogue with whom you meet is encouraged to sample elements of this book; such may assist in helping you to relate the symbolism of the liturgical experience to your life and see the mysteries of faith as your own.

During this Easter season of your life, reflect on what has happened to you in your conversion to Christ and initiation into the Church and its mysteries. Uncover the richness of the Sunday scriptures and reflect on their meaning for your life as you explore the liturgy of the vigil of Easter. Live, live, live as a disciple of Jesus Christ as you journey on your walk in the newness of life.

As noted earlier, you are called a "neophyte"—a newly baptized person. You are at a transition point on your walk of faith, a walk in which you need to continue to travel with the care and guidance of your parish community. But you are a traveler on a path you have not taken before. From all that prompted you to become a catechumen you have been on a journey of faith. You have traveled many roads since that time. Just as you traveled with others before your baptism and first sharing in the eucharist, so you continue your journey now with others. Those who previously were your help and guide now invite you to join them as members of the baptized on the ongoing journey of faith. So your journey continues, not alone, but alongside others in your parish to help you to stay the course in the opening days and weeks of Easter. Yes, you are a neophyte, but a neophyte in the midst of the parish community, not apart from it. Indeed, the road on which you journey is not a newly paved surface, but one with many layers of history under it. It is now *your* road to travel, maintain, and build with your parish.

Some Early Church Foundations

In the early Church, the period after baptism was one of immersion into the life of the community for the neophyte, the one made new. All during the spiritual journey, begun long before baptism and continued subsequent to it, the community had played an essential role in the candidate's preparation for and ultimate participation in the life of the Church. The time after baptism, therefore, occupied the rest of the lives of the neophytes, who were fully members of the faithful. The community to which the neophytes belonged, rooted in and sustained by the eucharist, survived, at least in part, by supporting one another and sharing one another's hardships.

Hippolytus of Rome, one of those responsible for the direction and development of the catechumenate in the early third century, noted that each neophyte was "to be zealous to perform good works and to please God, living righteously, devoting himself to the Church, performing the things which he has learnt, advancing in the service of God."[3] Another father of the Church, Origen, indicated that those to be baptized were now ready to be called "to our mysteries."[4]

The Acts of the Apostles provides several references to the believers' communal life (for example, 2:42–47; 4:32–37). Several early Church sources also note the manner in which the neophytes were cared for as members of the community.[5] They had experienced a lengthy formation before baptism—about three years[6]—and following baptism were quite naturally woven into the fabric of the worshiping community.

With the support of the Church community, coupled with the extensive preparation that had preceded baptism, the neophytes were well prepared to do their share in living and clinging firmly to the faith they called their own.

An Emerging Mystagogy

The issuance of the Edict of Constantine in A.D. 313 resulted in religious toleration, and once Christianity became legally permissible, risks associated with taking the name "Christian" dissipated. During the fourth and fifth centuries, the intensity of inquiry into the candidates' motives for baptism was not what it had been before. The major time of preparation for the sacraments of initiation came during the season of Lent. How different this was from the years of preparation during the second and third centuries.

Near the beginning of Lent, the catechumens who wished to pursue baptism indicated their desire by name; if accepted they became "the elect."[7] They experienced a formation in faith designed to support their approaching sacramental encounter. Their shortened preparation was enriched by ritual elements, such as frequent exorcisms; scrutinies fostered overcoming obstacles to living the Christian life. Michel Dujarier observes that, in addition to "catechetical lessons on Scripture and the Creed, some Churches also added catechesis on the Our Father. Toward the end of Lent, the two ceremonies called the 'traditions,' of giving the Creed and the Our Father to the baptismal candidates, took place."[8] Shaped by such preparation and formation in faith, the elect shared in the sacramental mysteries during the vigil of Easter. They were now able to join regularly the already baptized at the table of the eucharist.

What followed the events of the vigil was a week of heightened reflection on the mysteries entered into and shared—that enriching fashioning of faith called mystagogy. The neophytes would process to church during these days to hear the mysteries proclaimed with an especially rich vigor and love for the faith.[9] Having now experienced the sacraments of initiation, they heard with head and heart spiritual direction rooted in scriptural themes, exhortations to live a moral life, and exploration of the symbols and rites of initiation within the context of what they had experienced.[10]

How did the newly baptized respond to all that they heard? One answer comes to us from Egeria, a fourth-century nun from Spain, who had traveled to Jerusalem. She notes in her diary that the neophytes responded fervently and attentively to the bishop's teaching: "While the bishop discusses and explains each point, the applause is so loud that it can be heard even outside the church."[11]

In the fourth century, there emerged four Church fathers whose baptismal homilies were inspiring mystagogical presentations that enabled the neophytes to relate their own experience of the sacraments to the mysteries of initiation into the Church. These were Cyril of Jerusalem, Ambrose of Milan, John Chrysostom, and Theodore of Mopsuestia.[12] The work of these fathers can be described as the work of mystagogy. The presentation of biblical material, the exploration of symbols of the liturgy, the exhortations to live as a Christian occur within a framework that encompasses the neophytes' own life experience of the liturgical events.[13]

These fathers of the Church helped to keep the mysteries of faith alive despite a greatly abbreviated catechumenate. They took what they had—the liturgies of initiation—and provided a mystagogical interpretation. Selections from these preachers appear throughout this book as an aid to your own reflection. Perhaps what was proclaimed centuries ago can be a source of hope and confidence as you "and the local Church share the meaning of the initiatory mysteries and experience."[14]

For a variety of reasons the catechumenal linkage of rich liturgical expression with the initiatory experience of a gradual coming to faith began to dissolve. Not only decades, but centuries passed before a significant restoration would occur. Indeed, the restoration of the catechumenate has emerged during a time of intense liturgical renewal nearly 1400 years after its decline and 2000 years after the time of Christ. Not least in this ongoing renewal is the community's celebration of the paschal mystery during the Easter triduum.

The Easter Triduum and Beyond

One threshold of the experience of initiation occurs during the great Easter triduum during Holy Week. This triduum, or three days, begins on Holy Thursday with the evening eucharistic celebration of the Lord's Supper and concludes again in the evening, with prayer on Easter Sunday. This is the most solemn time of the Church year, with its high point coming during the Easter Vigil on Holy Saturday night. The Church gathers on Holy Thursday for the celebration of the eucharist, including the washing of the feet and transfer of the eucharist to a suitable place of repose. The liturgy moves into Good Friday with the liturgy of the word, veneration of the cross, and the communion service. No eucharistic liturgy is celebrated, however. Finally, on Holy Saturday, in addition to the preparation rites that may have occurred in the morning, the Church gathers for the great vigil: the service of light, the liturgy of the word, the celebration of baptism and confirmation, and the liturgy of the eucharist.

The Easter triduum itself is full of ritual action and symbolism. It ushers in the premier seasonal time to explore and discern with an Easter-consciousness the sacraments of baptism, confirmation, and the eucharist. Water, oil, blessings, anointings, candles, garments, signs and actions are not reminders of a distant God, but expressions of the awe-filled presence of the divine. You may "feel" closer to God in being splashed with water or anointed with oil. But you may also become a sign to others of what it means to live as a disciple of Christ as you unearth the meaning of the mysteries of faith through your experience of the sacraments.

The chapters that follow promote your coming to a heightened appreciation of the sacramental encounter. Such appreciation, though, is not merely a statement of what the sacraments of initiation mean. More than that, it is a discovery of what these sacraments are for you now in light of your experience of these dynamic signs of life and the presence of Christ. A neophyte may feel secure in the belief that the Holy Spirit moved him or her to come to faith; the same neophyte may also be convinced of the Spirit's call to encounter now the power and wonder of the sacred signs of the sacraments.

If your experience of the liturgical celebration and its accompanying symbols is one foundation for mystagogy, hearing and acting upon the power of the word in the lectionary is another. The Easter season Sunday readings, from Cycle A of the Church's three-year cycle, form the springboard for faith growth and reflection for the believing community during the period of mystagogy. These readings form the core scriptural component for each of the seven chapters of this book and correspond to the "Masses for neophytes, that is, the Sunday Masses of the Easter season" (*RCIA*, #247).[15]

The Lent-Easter events become more fully your own as you explore the great gospels and other biblical readings of the paschal season. For example, the gospels of resurrection, and of Christ as our way, truth, and life nurture your already lively faith. The Acts of the Apostles (the story of the new community) and the first letter of Peter (a postbaptismal message of support) complete the catechesis in word and sacrament.

The journey through the word that so richly captures the triduum experience is one that sustains and enriches the person about to be baptized. Review as often as you wish what you heard proclaimed during the three days. Refresh your memory with what you heard on Holy Thursday in the passover account of Moses and the Israelites. Note the language describing a lamb, the memorial feast, and the call to all generations to "celebrate with pilgrimage to the Lord, as a perpetual institution" (Exodus 12:14).[16]

Consider anew John's gospel account of Jesus' example of service in the washing of the feet of his disciples before the passover celebration. Read again slowly Paul's firm pronouncement to the community at Corinth: "I received from the Lord what I handed on to you, namely, that the Lord Jesus on the night in which he was betrayed took bread, and after he had given thanks, broke it and said, 'This is my body, which is for you. Do this in remembrance of me.' In the same way, after the supper, he took the cup, saying, 'This cup is the new covenant in my blood. Do this, whenever you drink it, in remembrance of me.' Every time, then, you eat this bread and drink this cup, you proclaim the death of the Lord until he comes!" (1 Corinthians 11:23–26).

Remember, too, to open the scriptures to the words of Isaiah proclaimed on Good Friday in which we are reminded of the suffering servant, the champion of justice, who "grew up like a sapling before him,/like a shoot from the parched earth;/There was in him no stately bearing to make us look at him,/nor appearance that would attract us to him" (Isaiah 53:2). Recall the great high priest described in the letter to the Hebrews, and create your own linkages to the passion account as presented in the gospel of John.

Finally, discover again the wealth of your tradition in the readings of the vigil. Enter into all the readings as you join the journey of faith and life of God's people over the ages. Seek new meanings in new beginnings in the first and second readings from Genesis, and enriched understandings from the journey of the Israelites "through the midst of the sea" (Exodus 14:29). Know the enduring love of your Maker in the fourth reading from Isaiah, and refresh yourself with the words of the same prophet in the fifth reading: "All you who are thirsty,/come to the water!" (Isaiah 55:1). Meditate on the treasures of wisdom from the prophet Baruch: "She [Wisdom] is the book of the precepts of God,/the law that endures forever" (Baruch 4:1). Seal the experience of the Old yet ever so current Testament with reassuring words from Ezekiel the prophet: "I will give you a new heart and place a new spirit within you" (Ezekiel 36:26).

As you focus on the vigil's New Testament proclamations, consider again the words of Paul to the Romans reminding you that you are baptized into Christ's death: "Through baptism into his death we were buried with him, so that, just as Christ was raised from the dead by the glory of the Father, we too might live a new life" (Romans 6:4). A fitting conclusion to such a scripture meditation is the gospel reading from the vigil, in which you heard proclaimed one of the accounts of the women disciples at the tomb of Jesus. For example, Matthew's account tells us they hear of Jesus being raised up and are charged to go tell the disciples: "He has been raised from the dead and now goes ahead of you to Galilee, where you will see him" (Matthew 28:7). (See also Mark 16:1–8 or Luke 24:1–12.)

Your walk in the newness of life is a timeless journey, one that will call you to discern again and again the power of the scriptures of the triduum as your life progresses. Surely, do not feel compelled to review them all now! However, do review them periodically and at your own pace as you continue to shape the story of faith you call your own. They are listed here to assist you whenever you choose to rediscover their meaning for your life.

Holy Thursday
Exodus 12:1–8, 11–14
1 Corinthians 11:23–26
John 13:1–15

Good Friday
Isaiah 52:13—53:12
Hebrews 4:14–16; 5:7–9
John 18:1—19:42

Easter Vigil
Genesis 1:1—2:2
Genesis 22:1–18
Exodus 14:15—15:1
Isaiah 54:5–14
Isaiah 55:1–11
Baruch 3:9–15, 32—4:4
Ezekiel 36:16–28
Romans 6:3–11
Matthew 28:1–10

The Eucharistic Celebration

The summit of the mystagogical experience is the eucharistic celebration. In sharing eucharist with the already baptized, you join with your sisters and brothers in faith in demonstrating that all "are one body, for we all partake of the one loaf" (1 Corinthians 10:17). Gathered with other believers, you share in the offering at the table of the eucharist. Your gifts of bread and wine become gifts of the Father to be shared among the entire assembly as the body and blood of Christ.

The eucharist is emphasized throughout this book. It is the only sacrament of initiation to be repeated, enabling the baptized to gather and celebrate at least weekly the mystery they proclaim daily in their lives of work, family, play, struggle, joy and peacemaking. The weekly gathering for eucharist provides a reentry into the sharing of the mysteries—to be comprehended, though incompletely, through the words and actions of the already baptized. Meeting and praying with members of the parish, engaging in parish ministries, discussing the mysteries of faith through the lens of liturgical and initiation experiences—all contribute to one's growth in the mysteries.

This growth to which you are called is not one-sided, however. The parish and its mystagogue(s) guide you and assist you in relating the symbolism of the liturgical experience to the story of your life. Your story of life, begun long before you became a catechumen, continues in new and surprising ways as you reflect upon the events of Easter and uncover the consequences of your decision to pass through the water to the table of the Lord.

Renewing the Parish

How fortunate that you do not experience mystagogy alone! Your baptism is a positive sign to those baptized before you of value, of worth, of faith. As they pause to witness what you are becoming, they begin to verify, confirm, or modify their own directions in life. They are challenged—by your acceptance of what others might perhaps take for granted—to reflect on their own experiences of font and table. Perhaps some even ask themselves whom they worship anyway or why they assemble on Sunday. Some may respond by "carrying" you into the deeper life of the parish and its many ministries. Others may witness and issue through one another's voices a challenge to speak and act on the gospel. They may even explore for the first time what they themselves have really witnessed.

Through the time of postbaptismal catechesis, "the neophytes, with the help of their godparents, should experience a full and joyful welcome into the community and enter into closer ties with the other faithful. The faithful, in turn, should derive from it a renewal of inspiration and of outlook" (*RCIA*, #246).[17]

You may be the "paschal transfusion" that may be just what's needed to revitalize the parish's mission. You may be the fresh breath that clears the air and blows coolly in the direction of parish ministries and organizations in need of renewal. Made in the image and likeness of God and reborn in the death-resurrection of Jesus, you are fully part of the community which served as the vehicle of your birth. You take your place alongside the already baptized. Together you are called to meditate on the gospel, share the eucharist, and engage in charitable works.

Your participation alongside the other faithful may unite the parish's ministerial efforts and promote renewal of parish organizations. During the mystagogical period, you can expand your horizons beyond the parish itself. Ministry from the parish to the surrounding social community is one important and sometimes forgotten dimension of Christian responsibility. The extent to which you respond to broader community needs is, in part, a function of the vision of parish that has been promoted and lived all during the catechumenal process. Our bishops tell us that "the social mission of the parish begins in the gospel's call to conversion; to change our hearts and our lives; to follow in the path of charity, justice, and peace. The parish is the place we should regularly hear the call to conversion and find help in answering the Lord's call to express our faith in concrete acts of charity and justice."[18]

Finally, your prayer life, strengthened by prayer with Christian initiation team members and the parish at large, is to be developed further. Prayer was an essential dimension of coming to faith all during your catechumenal preparation. Then and now your parish prays as one in union with the risen Lord. The return of the parish to prayer—of thanks, of petition, of mercy, of praise—is a fervent sign of the impact of the conversion process on the community of believers. It is, really, a realization that as we live and pray together, and find within the presence of God in our lives, we find each other. Conversion to Christ becomes a transformation of others insofar as each of us is already transformed in the Spirit of Christ. Such is the challenge and call of the Lord and movement of the Spirit as witnessed in our day in the life of the neophyte.

The baptized community of the faithful and the neophytes participate together in a common journey, sharing in a variety of parish ministries. With such participation and mutual enrichment, the parish can move forward, secure in its mission to spread the Good News and live by its demands.

It is hoped that this book will assist you to get behind the symbols of the liturgy of initiation, to see connections with the scriptures of the Easter season, and to come to see mystagogy as not just fifty days of the season, ending on Pentecost, but the time that follows as well. While it is recommended that you gather monthly until the first anniversary of your baptism, your weekly parish gathering for eucharist can be for years to come a renewal of your first sharing in the paschal mystery of Jesus' passion, death, and resurrection.

As you continue to face challenges in your life, you may be finding yourself examining passions, deaths, and resurrection experiences you have had. What passion do you bring to your faith? What deaths do you suffer through? What risings in life are yours to share? Allow the limited time of the Easter season to be a springboard for all that you may face in the future.

Performing works of charity is a critical dimension of the experience of the neophyte. This is not to suggest that you have suddenly become a charitable person, somehow suggesting that you were not so inclined before. Rather, it is to affirm that the one who lives through eucharist is called to bring that eucharistic sense of living to others; the foundation, then, for such living is one's sharing in the eucharist. The eucharist is strength for the baptized, enabling and empowering you to be strength for others.

Allow the symbols of the eucharist to be symbols that lead you to affirm or change what you do. Enable them to be symbols that empower you to reach out to others with a healing hand and hearing heart. Recognize your freedom to be with your parish the body of Christ to others, encouraging, loving, identifying with them. Know the justice of God and promote it through your hands, eyes, and ears every day. Foster peaceful living in your parish, your work place, your home. Under it all, cherish the eucharist as the source of your resolve, moving you to become a faithful traveler as you walk in the newness of life.

Mystagogy, then, can be for you a sacred pause, the start of the longer and perhaps more challenging story of initiation—one's life beyond the font of baptism. Each time the eucharist is celebrated, the baptismal experience of all assembled is renewed, regained, and reasserted. The story of each is remembered, strengthened, and retold by the story of all the faithful.

How to Use This Book

Each chapter of this book focuses on a Sunday in the Easter season. Within each of the chapters are four major parts:

Exploring Your Experience
Exploring the Scriptures
Renewing Your Life of Faith
Accepting the Challenge

Each of the four parts enables you to immerse yourself in a chapter theme from a variety of perspectives. For example, *Exploring Your Experience* provides a brief description of the chapter theme along with questions to help you determine how the theme relates to your life. *Exploring the Scriptures* seeks to provide a dialogue between biblical material and your reflections on the scriptural readings as related to the overall chapter. *Renewing Your Life of Faith* develops further the theme with presentation of liturgical elements, often in relation to fourth century mystagogical teaching. You can see how the material presented thus far in each chapter might have an impact on your life, and what you might do to put into practice what you have experienced. Finally, *Accepting the Challenge* helps you to decide how you might act on what has been discovered as a result of your reading and reflection.

Each chapter begins with a psalm-prayer, just before the chapter overview. These psalms coincide with the readings of the Sundays presented here and provide a prayerful mode of entry into the flow of the chapters.

There is also a *Did You Know?* entry at the end of each chapter's *Renewing Your Life of Faith* section. These entries focus on a variety of topics pertinent to Christian initiation. The last such entry, in chapter 7, deals with Pentecost. The celebration of Pentecost provides the believing community with a model of enlivened faith and determined resolve to live in the Spirit of God. Pentecost is a day of challenge for the Church, a day that calls the faithful to live what they believe all year long.

While Pentecost represents the formal close to the Easter season, it also can be seen as a bridge to the Church's Ordinary Time, a time in which you and your parish are to demonstrate that "there are different kinds of spiritual gifts but the same Spirit; there are different forms of service but the same Lord; there are different workings but the same God who produces all of them in everyone" (1 Corinthians 12:4–6). As you conclude chapter 7 of this book, try to discern the promptings of the Holy Spirit moving you and your parish to work together for the good of all. Such ministry together might just become the seed of a "living chapter" for your common life in Christ.

To aid your reflection, there are varieties of questions and suggested activities throughout each of the chapters. Use these as you wish; some may appeal to you more than others. They are intended to help you go deeper, to uncover what lies behind your experience of coming to faith, and may assist in your dialogue with parishioners, a parish mystagogue, a godparent, or others on the initiation team. Indeed, dialogue with others all during your use of this book can result in an enriched postbaptismal experience.

As a newly baptized person, you are called to see differently now—and to see with eyes of faith along with the already baptized. Accept the challenge of being a Church that embraces, engaging others in a conversion that replenishes and sustains, listens and calls forth. Be the Church of Jesus Christ, the Church of bonding with others in your parish, yourself part of the nets of the scriptures, soaked in the water of new birth, stretched to the breaking point, yet holding fast together.

Seize the power of the graced moments of the triduum and surge ahead to Christian mission, accompanied by your parish's vision of its own renewal through these same waters and simple table. Shaped by the word, nourished by the eucharist, serve together as disciples of the Lord and savior of all. Saturate this earth with a new witness, and a dynamic faith that is crisp, bright, and beckoning you to union with the divine. Make this journey confident that word and sacrament are well served by your response to the Church's call to mission.

Walk always in the newness of life—and become that newness of life to others. May your sacred pause enable you to be for others what those before you have been for you—a link in the journey of faith enriched by your own conversion to Christ and enlivened through your sharing in the worship and life of the community of the Church.

1

The Challenge of Your Life of Faith

PSALM–PRAYER

Give thanks to the LORD, who is good,
    whose love endures forever.
Let the house of Israel say:
    God's love endures forever....

    "The LORD's right hand is raised;
    the LORD's right hand strikes with power."
I shall not die but live
    and declare the deeds of the LORD....

    The stone the builders rejected
        has become the cornerstone.
    By the LORD has this been done;
        it is wonderful in our eyes.

Psalm 118:1–2, 16–17, 22–23

Overview

Congratulations on becoming baptized! You may feel both exhilarated and exhausted as you ponder all that led you to seek initiation into the Church.

Your preparation for baptism included a variety of rites and liturgical celebrations, intended to help you strengthen your faith and prepare for the great celebration of baptism. In this first chapter you have the opportunity to explore the challenge of your life of faith in light of your experience of seeking to be baptized within the community of faith.

You will see some terms as you explore all that follows that may not appear to be clearly defined for you—for example, challenge, mystery, conversion, trust. These and other words do not carry with them exact definitions here—and that's all right. It is hoped that understanding of these and other terms will emerge as you use this book, helping you to shape their meaning for *your* life.

Throughout this book are questions for you to think about and space for jotting down your thoughts. Respond as often as you wish. In addition, dialogue with your godparent(s), other newly baptized persons, or family members who can strengthen your experience of Christian living after baptism. Now please begin, and explore your experience of becoming a Christian, a disciple of the risen Lord.

EXPLORING YOUR EXPERIENCE

Astronauts marvel at planet earth from distant, endless skies...

Artists try to capture the breadth of the sea in the images they put to canvas...

Astronauts, artists, all of us...somehow facing challenges that may lead us in new directions!

As you looked forward to your baptism, you may have been challenged to explore your ongoing conversion in faith. Perhaps you sensed a new direction.

- What do the two images of the world and the seascape say to you about challenges in your life? How do you "view the earth" from where you live or work? What challenges do you face daily?

____

____

____

____

- What picture would you "paint" of your experience of the catechumenate and your baptism? Draw or write about it here.

The following quotation from one-fourth century preacher addresses the challenge of the baptismal life this way:

Great is the prize set before you in Baptism: ransom for captives, remission of sin, death of sin, a new, spiritual birth, a shining garment, a holy seal inviolable, a Heaven-bound chariot, delights of Paradise, a passport to the Kingdom, the grace of the adoption of sons. But a dragon lies in ambush for the traveler....

With Hope invincible for your sandals and with Faith the guest of your heart, you may pass through the enemy's lines and enter into the house of the Lord. Prepare your heart for the reception of teaching and the fellowship in the holy Mysteries. Pray more frequently, that God may count you worthy of the heavenly and eternal Mysteries....

May He fill you with the heavenly treasures of the New Covenant and sign you with that seal of the Holy Spirit which no man shall break forever, in Christ Jesus our Lord, to whom be glory forever and ever. Amen.[1]

This passage, by Cyril of Jerusalem (and translated in anything but modern English), reminds those to be baptized of the challenge before them.

One might get the impression that, in approaching baptism, the believer had to be prepared for any kind of obstacle: "a dragon lies in ambush for the traveler." Language used today is not, some might say, as rich or symbolic as that of this fourth-century preacher. However, the deeper meaning of the images themselves may cause people to pause and think about what may lie in ambush for them today. Passive acceptance of the status quo in a struggling marriage may lead to an eventual breakup. What began as a challenging career may quietly turn into a routine job. Indifference to AIDS tragically results in an unstoppable epidemic. Lack of concern for or ambivalence toward the exposure of children to an increasingly violent society leads to confusion and denials of accountability.

This chapter, and the ones that follow, have been written to help you go beneath the surface of the obvious meaning of events in your life. You may be asked to explore times when you felt "ambushed"—when you felt cornered or challenged and needed help to find your way through a difficult situation or strained relationship. For now, try to think of one example from your life when you felt "cornered." What was it? How did you respond to it? Why do you think you responded the way you did?

____

____

____

____

Changes in our lives may help us to establish our identity. People do not all of a sudden become adults. Rather, people "grow into" their adulthood. You may be challenged to come to see for yourself who you are and what you are all about. For example, you may have to choose between two good jobs: What do you do? How do you choose? Or, you may decide to support a candidate or political position that is generally unpopular. What do you do now?

People mature and change, move through the hills and valleys and ups and downs of life, and experience a greater sense of where they are headed as they respond to life's challenges. Through it all, people may sense that they are, indeed, their own best resource for meeting life's challenges. Continue now your own search by reading and thinking about your baptism.

During your preparation for baptism, you may have been challenged to describe your ongoing conversion in faith. If you were so challenged, just what was this challenge for you?

____

____

____

____

Sometimes people need to renounce or rid themselves of something in facing a new challenge, particularly when reaching a transition point in their lives. They may have to let go of some past habit or behavior, or alter or terminate a relationship in approaching a new challenge. Ask yourself:

- What were my feelings as I thought about becoming Catholic? Did my choice involve a relationship with another person? How?

____

____

____

____

In the chart that follows name one or more challenges you have had to face in your life. For each of them, indicate whether you found yourself needing to give up something in facing the challenge. Use the space provided to record what you gave up. Then identify how you might face such a challenge in the future.

Life's Challenges

Challenges I Have Faced	*I Gave Up*	*I Might Face Challenges in the Future by*
1.		
2.		
3.		

Now answer these questions for one or more of the experiences above. You may also wish to discuss them with others.

- Did the experience serve as a "transition" experience, or passage, from one period of life to another? How?

____

____

____

____

- Was it difficult to let go of whatever you gave up? Why or why not?

____

____

____

____

Challenge and Faith

Baptism presents an opportunity to say most positively, "Yes, I believe!" Just as you were asked to renounce evil at your baptism, so, too, you were encouraged to profess what you believed. You were given the opportunity to affirm your commitment to a Christian way of life and what it meant to you. One newly baptized person has remarked:

> I felt that I had no roots or background in another religion to say goodbye to and I felt like everything I was doing was saying yes to everything I wanted. This is something I wanted for years....I didn't feel like I was giving up anything, I felt like I was just gaining so much.

Another states: "[As baptism approached] I was not really afraid of anything; I was more excited than anything!"

What people believe in can help them to face life's challenges. Consider for a moment the virtue of faith. You have professed the faith of the Church and are now bound more closely to those baptized before you. Together, you are *faithful*. The gift of faith permeates one's whole personal attitude, an attitude that focuses not only on knowing beliefs, but also on trusting in God and acting according to one's convictions in the day-to-day affairs of life. In this sense, faith has to do with relationships, emotions, one's will and the intellect. It involves one's whole attitude toward God and one's notion of what it means to communicate with others in the world. To be people of faith is to be engaged in a search that can become richer and deeper as life goes on.

Faith calls people to a certain way of living as well as believing. It can be seen as a gift from God that shapes people's identity as Christians. In choosing to identify yourself with others as a baptized Christian, you have chosen to opt for a particular way of living. You even may have had to say goodbye to certain things that were preventing you from living a way of life shaped by the gospel of Jesus.

Your life as a person of faith may undergo challenge and change in the years ahead. For now, consider what your life might have been like had you not chosen to pursue the Christian faith. In what way do you think it might have been different from what it is now? The same?

____

____

____

____

Reflect on why you risk the challenge of a life of faith with others. What's in it for you? How do you feel about professing your faith? Why?

____

____

____

____

Look back at the challenges you listed on page 23. What were your feelings as you faced one or more of them? How do you feel about looking back on them?

____

____

____

____

EXPLORING THE SCRIPTURES

People often need strength and support as they try to live lives of faith. The challenge of living a life of faith is not some simple task. It can be tough to live as a person of faith. Perhaps you chose to experience the catechumenate to strengthen your relationship with Jesus and your local parish community. Perhaps you wanted to find support for your decision to inquire about becoming Catholic.

One person, in looking back on her experience of the catechumenate, notes:

> I was never familiar with a group of people like this. I knew most of the people would really have deep faith and a lot of feeling toward the Church ...and here was this stranger...not intruding, but in a way I felt like I was going into something I knew nothing about...and I really enjoyed going.

Your baptism may have taken place during the great liturgy of the Easter Vigil, the highlight of the entire Church year. If it did, you experienced for the first time the complete Easter celebration, rich in symbols of light and sound, gesture and smell. Perhaps the service of light and the liturgies of word, baptism, and eucharist all flowed together for you in one great celebration—indeed, this special moment of your initiation into the Catholic Church.

One newly baptized parishioner remarked in recalling her baptism: "My feelings during the Easter Vigil were filled with excitement! I felt proud to be a member of such a loving Church. I felt no one could take this away from me." Another newly baptized person adds:

> What were my feelings during the Easter Vigil? I was really excited, I was ecstatic. . . . I just had this feeling that, afterwards when we got together and we talked about it, I was just in oblivion. I didn't really see a lot of the things that happened!

As you continue to use this book, think back from time to time to your parish's celebration of your baptism to help you identify its meaning for your life. But do not limit your thinking only to recall the parts of the liturgy. Focus, too, on your emotions at that time and on your response as a "whole person of faith" as you moved toward baptism, as you were finally immersed, as you were anointed with chrism, and as you joined in the eucharist with your parish for the first time. For now, ask yourself:

- How did the symbols of the celebration affect me?

____

____

____

____

- What did my experience of being in that church at that hour of the night, with other believers, mean to me? (Use the space below to record your thoughts, or draw a symbol that represents the way you felt.)

During the time before baptism you were asked if you rejected sin and were willing to profess your faith. As you read on, recall some experiences from your life that led you to join the Church. These may help you to reflect on the scriptures that follow, and their meaning for your life today.

The Scriptures of Easter Sunday

The readings for this first Sunday of the Easter season are from the Acts of the Apostles, the letter of Paul to the Colossians, and the gospel according to John.

ACTS OF THE APOSTLES 10:34, 37–43

The first reading addresses, in part, being willing to share with others one's experience of and belief in Jesus. The word "witness" might be used to describe this. People may witness by volunteering their time in a parish human services center. Or they may witness by helping young people identify for themselves what they value in life. (Perhaps the challenge of this type of witness is that of support as the young person makes informed personal choices.) As you read this passage, think of ways you can witness to what you believe in.

Peter addressed the people in these words: "I take it you know what has been reported all over Judea about Jesus of Nazareth, beginning in Galilee with the baptism John preached; of the way God anointed him with the Holy Spirit and power. He went about doing good works and healing all who were in the grip of the devil, and God was with him. We are witnesses to all that he did in the land of the Jews and in Jerusalem. They killed him finally, 'hanging him on a tree,' only to have God raise him up on the third day and grant that he be seen, not by all, but only by such witnesses as had been chosen beforehand by God—by us who ate and drank with him after he rose from the dead. He commissioned us to preach to the people and to bear witness that he is the one set apart by God as judge of the living and the dead. To him all the prophets testify, saying that everyone who believes in him has forgiveness of sins through his name."

This reading is Peter's last great discourse, during which he announces the good news of Jesus Christ to the gentile centurion Cornelius and to Cornelius' family and friends. Peter asserts his faith and that of the other disciples in the risen Jesus. He summarizes the account of Jesus' anointing by the Holy Spirit and Jesus' death and resurrection. The message first given to the Jews is now brought to the gentiles. Peter's words challenge people to believe in Jesus and to reject sin in their lives. For both Jewish Christians and for gentiles who were soon to be baptized, belief in the risen Jesus was of great importance: God granted "that he be seen, not by all, but only...by us who ate and drank with him after he rose from the dead" (verses 40–41). The author of the Acts of the Apostles goes on to describe the coming of the Holy Spirit upon the gentiles, before their baptism with water. Pause now and ask yourself:

- How do I seek to know God? Am I like Cornelius, still eager to hear about this Jesus?

- How does Peter's preaching to the gentiles help me to understand God as a God of all people? How do I feel about that?

- How do I feel about people of other religious persuasions? Why is that?

Colossians 3:1–4

The second reading, from Paul, encourages the Christian not to lose sight of Christ as the center of one's life. At work, at home, alone, with others—how you act and your attitude toward life can be influenced by your belief in Jesus the Christ. Paul himself said: "For to me life is Christ and death is gain" (Philippians 1:21).

Since you have been raised up in company with Christ, set your heart on what pertains to higher realms where Christ is seated at God's right hand. Be intent on things above rather than on things of earth. After all, you have died! Your life is hidden now with Christ in God. When Christ our life appears, then you shall appear with him in glory.

This passage was written while Paul was under house arrest in Rome, a few years after his third missionary journey. He was eager to clarify the exalted place of Christ in Christian belief and to respond to what he believed were false teachings coming out of Colossae. Indeed, Paul provides a precise guideline for living one's life in accord with that of Christ: Christ is to be the central point, or turning point, for a Christian, like you, who has symbolically died with Christ and who is intent on rising again with him. This is a central baptismal teaching, so that all who are baptized may live in the fullness of life: life with God.

This second reading should not be used in a narrow way. For example, one might be tempted to think solely in terms of "me and Jesus," thereby ignoring broad and important issues of justice and other concerns of today's world such as ageism, racism, and sexism, that need attention and work. Christians are called to accept the transforming power of Christian baptism—certainly, with Christ at its center—and proceed to live in ways that can help to overcome local, regional, and world evils. Christians need to work to eliminate the sin in their own lives as they seek to rid society of all sorts of injustices.

It seems right to pause here to enable you to reflect on one or more of the following questions. As with many of the reflection opportunities in this book, you might choose to share some of these questions with your godparent(s) or one or two other companions, leading to an enriched reflection for all.

- Do you sometimes try to escape from reality by only being "intent on things above" in a narrow sense? Why? What might people of faith do to face such questions as violence, human rights, economic and ecology issues?

____

____

____

____

- Are there people you know or have heard about who have taken risks in living by their beliefs? Why might they take the risks? What risks might you have to take to live by what you believe? Why?

____

____

____

____

- What are your feelings about working with all people, including people from other religions?

____

____

____

____

- Do you feel that your relationship with Jesus is a separate issue from your relationship with others? Explain.

____

____

____

____

- Name... one local issue
  one national issue
  one global issue...
  that you feel is a problem. What can be done to address this issue? How might your parish start?

____

____

____

____

JOHN 20:1–9

The gospel reading challenges Christians to reflect on the meaning of Jesus' resurrection for their lives. For example, how does Jesus' resurrection encourage Christians to live as people of hope? As people who are willing to take risks for what they believe is the right thing to do?

Early in the morning on the first day of the week, while it was still dark, Mary Magdalene came to the tomb. She saw that the stone had been moved away, so she ran off to Simon Peter and the other disciple (the one Jesus loved) and told them, "The Lord has been taken from the tomb! We don't know where they have put him!" At that, Peter and the other disciple started out on their way toward the tomb. They were running side by side, but then the other disciple outran Peter and reached the tomb first. He did not enter but bent down to peer in, and saw the wrappings lying on the ground and saw the piece of cloth which had covered the head not lying with the wrappings, but rolled up in a place by itself. Then the disciple who had arrived first at the tomb went in. He saw and believed. (Remember, as yet they did not understand the Scripture that Jesus had to rise from the dead.)

The time is before dawn on Easter Sunday morning. Mary Magdalene, a disciple of Jesus, observes the empty tomb and alerts Peter and the disciple whom Jesus loved especially. Note the responsiveness of the beloved disciple to what he sees. The gospel writer states simply: "He saw and believed." The writer did not demean Peter's faith, but rather elevated the position of the beloved disciple, the one who sat close to Jesus at the Last Supper (John 13:23–25).

The beloved disciple is one who both sees and believes. He gives us an example of one who expresses powerful love unconditionally. The disciple sees the burial cloths in the empty tomb and believes that Jesus is risen. He comes to a heightened faith in the one he loved and served. Some scholars contrast the faith of the beloved disciple to that of Thomas the apostle, who sought a special sign from Jesus following the resurrection (John 20:25), and thus did not show his faith quickly.

Through the empty tomb, Christians have for centuries "seen" and believed in the risen Jesus. By what they have not visibly seen, Christians have, through faith, believed in Jesus and his raising from death to life.

One core teaching of Christian faith is Jesus' death and resurrection. This mystery, called the paschal mystery, is an essential focus of Catholic belief. Jesus does not only live again, but is raised from death in a way no person can completely comprehend. Yet by discovering what it means to live as a Christian in the world one may be able to begin to live out the consequences of the resurrection. In rising from death, Jesus provides a hope for meeting the challenges that confront people and that can prevent them from becoming their best selves. Christians are to live in the spirit of the resurrection.

You can continue to reject evil and profess your faith just as you did at your baptism, now by your words and actions. Your faith in the resurrection of Jesus can become a dynamic, active expression of strengthened belief, heightened trust, and decisive resolve to act as a follower of Christ. This faith you profess, then, is not only some single body of truths, but a developing sense of what you are called to become as a baptized member of the Church. It is a challenge to see in the uncertainty of life hope for the future. It is a search for life's goodness and for what unites rather than divides, heals rather than hurts, and trusts rather than denies. Reflect now on the following, either alone or with others.

- Name some experience that led to a renewed sense of hope for your life. Do you sometimes want to "see" everything clearly in a work or home relationship before you are willing to believe, to trust, to hope? Why is that?

___

___

___

___

- What does it mean for you to believe, to be and become a person of faith? What everyday event in your life might remind you of your faith in God?

- What are the most important points, in your opinion, of the last two sections of this chapter, "Exploring Your Experience" and "Exploring the Scriptures"? How do you think they will influence you? What will you do the same? Differently?

RENEWING YOUR LIFE OF FAITH

One source for helping you to renew your life of faith professed at baptism is sermons of fathers of the Church delivered around the time of Easter. Speaking in the fourth century, these preachers helped their listeners explore the meaning of the baptismal events, often in the days following Easter. Their words are meant to help you now.

Such preachers as Ambrose of Milan and Cyril of Jerusalem revealed nothing about the Easter celebration to catechumens preparing for baptism. Only in the days following this liturgy did they explore with the newly baptized, called neophytes, the meaning of the mysteries of faith they had experienced. These fathers would encourage their listeners to reflect on the scriptures and on their experience of the whole baptismal celebration.

The fathers spoke of a highly symbolic renunciation of sin and profession of faith. For example, Cyril had the candidate stand, face west, which was considered the source of darkness, and say: "I renounce you, Satan.... and all your works.... and all his pomp.... and all your service."[2] Similarly, Ambrose of Milan reminded the newly baptized: "You renounced the Devil and his works, the world with its luxury and pleasures. Your words are kept not in the tomb of the dead, but in the book of the living."[3]

The rejection of the devil was of great importance to these preachers and to their audiences. In vivid and symbolic language, the fathers addressed the devil's pursuit of the candidates for baptism and the necessity to break the power of the evil one. Satan symbolized all that would prevent one from seeking union with Christ and from living no longer as a slave to whatever would hinder movement toward God.

Today, people's enslavements may be understood in broader terms as well. True, your own renunciation of evil and profession of faith were clear expressions of your decision to proceed to baptism. You were asked if you freely rejected sin, the glamor of evil, and the prince of darkness. Your brief response, perhaps with the words "I do," may have been a firm statement of your decision to sever any remaining bonds that might prevent your committing yourself to Christ.

If you go beneath the surface of your thoughts, however, you might discover additional understandings for rejecting evil and the "prince of darkness" today. Awareness of local, national, and global concerns is a sharp reminder of all the evil that exists. Look around the block, or around the world through a satellite-fed TV screen, and observe what wrongs need to be righted, what sinful attitudes might be corrected. What a challenge!

Take a look at...

- hunger in the United States, including millions of children living in poverty in this country;
- starvation in drought-stricken areas of Africa;
- the spiraling movement toward violent solutions to family and neighborhood problems;
- subtle discrimination in cities and towns;
- and so on...

and you get a picture of contemporary goings-on that must be rejected and overcome. Today's evils also may be personified in movements and ideologies, such as exaggerated and unjust nationalism. Evil remains in many ways a mystery of its own that cannot be addressed only by social programs and projects. As Paul's letter to the Ephesians points out: "For our struggle is not with flesh and blood but with the principalities, with the powers, with the world rulers of this present darkness, with the evil spirits in the heavens" (6:12). Still, in acting to overcome evils you may be aware of, you enter your name in the "book of the living," and commit yourself to the work of the prince of peace.

- Do you see evils where you live that need to be overcome? If so, what might you do to help?

____

____

____

____

Professing Faith: Then and Now

Consider for a moment the following practice of the fourth century and how wonderful it must have been, after all the statements and gestures of rejecting sin, finally to profess one's faith. "Faith is the eye that enlightens every conscience and produces understanding,"[4] Cyril of Jerusalem told candidates for baptism a few weeks before their profession of faith on Holy Saturday night. Then, in sharing truths of faith with the candidates, Cyril urged them:

> This summary I wish you to commit to memory, word for word, and to repeat among yourselves with all zeal, not writing it on paper, but engraving it by memory on the heart.... Keep it as a provision for the way throughout the whole course of your life.[5]

Cyril is helping the candidates to view their faith not only as a statement of beliefs, but also as a guidepost for living a Christian life. Each candidate's whole attitude, whole life, was to be shaped by the individual's commitment to the way of Christ. Some weeks later, Cyril would use the following words to help the newly baptized think back to their profession of faith. Notice the bodily turning from west to east, symbolic of one's conversion:

> God's paradise opens before you, that Eden, planted in the east, from which for his transgression our first father was banished. Symbolic of this is your facing about from the west to the east, the place of light. It was at this point that you were told to say: "I believe in the Father, and in the Son, and in the Holy Spirit, and in one Baptism of repentance."[6]

Having professed their faith, the candidates moved closer to their immersion in the waters of baptism. What joy they must have felt in anticipation of what was to come!

Your profession of faith was not only a verbal statement, but an important and essential expression of your acceptance of the core belief of the Church. It should not have been a "once and for all" expression, to be remembered only as part of a nice church celebration. Rather, it is an expression of enduring belief, of a faith nurtured by the word of God and made ready for challenges you may face. It is something that you can and should review often.

Think now of what you believe in, of what you really value about your decision to become Catholic. Ask yourself:

- Do my relationships with others have anything to do with my life of faith? Why or why not?

- What does it mean for me to say:

  —that I believe in myself?

  —that I believe in the presence of God in my life?

—that I believe in Jesus?

____

____

____

____

—that I believe in and identify with the Church?

____

____

____

____

Did You Know?

In the fourth century, one of the highlights of the symbolic events before baptism was the anointing of the candidate. These various anointings had several meanings, including:

- belonging to Christ
- lifetime union with Christ
- triumph over sin
- purifying and healing
- commitment to Christ

You may have experienced one or more anointings with the oil of catechumens during the catechumenate. These anointings symbolized your strengthening by God and becoming strong in faith—being able to face whatever might challenge your life as a Christian. The oil itself is a symbol of preservation and of strength. In a sense, by seeking baptism, you accepted the challenge of discovering what the Christian faith means to you. Your anointing with oil was a way for the Church community, your parish, to offer from its own faith its prayer and willingness to help maintain your life of faith. The community prayed that you be strengthened in Christ and be freed from whatever might prevent you from living as a Christian.

The most important anointing of all, however, came after baptism. This was the anointing with the oil of chrism, used in the celebration of confirmation. (More on confirmation appears in chapters 2 and 6.) All who gathered with you at the time of your baptism may have prayed as one for the outpouring of the Spirit in your life. The priest may have said to the group:

> My dear friends, let us pray to God our Father, that he will pour out the Holy Spirit on these newly baptized to strengthen them with his gifts and anoint them to be more like Christ, the Son of God (*RCIA*, #233).[7]

- For now, think back to times when you were anointed. What were your feelings as the minister touched you with the oil?

____

____

____

____

- Now look at the list of anointing meanings above. Choose one of them and reflect on how it might help you to face challenges in your life—to live according to what you believe.

____

____

____

____

ACCEPTING THE CHALLENGE

Water, oil, gestures: all are important symbols for the newly baptized. More important, however, is your own discovery of what these symbols, and your profession of faith, now mean to you as a baptized Christian. Perhaps you will come to see that the most appropriate baptismal symbol is your life as a person of faith. Your faith matured during the catechumenate as you prepared to be baptized in the faith of the Church. This active faith now calls you to do what you can to render justice where necessary, correction when called upon, and love for all.

The consequences of your baptism are, in a sense, what you make of them. Your baptism and all you did in preparation for it can become a pleasant memory of a refreshing time in your life. It also can become a source for continuing to grow into your baptism, as you discover that your journey of faith has only just begun. Baptized in water and the Spirit, you are challenged now to risk—yes, risk—living out your baptism. You are challenged to risk professing your faith, and to risk rejecting whatever would prevent you from being and becoming a person of justice and peace.

The central question to ask yourself now, and, if you wish, to discuss with others, is: What does all this have to do with my life? What does my profession of faith have to do with challenges I am facing right now?

As a member of the Church, you enjoy the support of others who also have been baptized. Whether your fellow parishioners were baptized as children or adults, they all belong to a parish community that shares a common heritage and identity as a Church formed by the word of God. In seeking baptism, you have entered into this heritage, becoming a part of the Church's own story of faith. In a real way, your personal story of faith is now part of the Church's story, and vice versa.

Imagine for a moment that you were not baptized into your parish, but into a church of individuals with no real sense of responsibility for one another. What might this be like? How might you feel?

____

____

____

____

Now imagine moving into a parish in which many parish leaders or other parishioners seemed uninterested in developing an active lively faith. How would this make you feel? What might you do to improve the situation?

____

____

____

____

Discuss the above two situations with others if you wish.

Looking Back

Enter now more deeply into the mystery of your own baptism. Focus for a few moments on what led you to profess your faith before your immersion in the waters of rebirth.

Review briefly some of the main points of the sections on the scriptures (pages 26-36) and renewing your life of faith (pages 36-43). As you do, consider what has challenged you or what you wish to move beyond. Perhaps there are levels of understanding you have reached that would move you beyond the meanings you see here. For example, you may have a new insight into some specific difficulties you face daily. You may want to take a new look at one or more relationships in your life. Or you may be struggling with a moral issue, and something in this chapter may have triggered some new alternatives for you.

The goal here is to try to sharpen your awareness of your whole attitude toward God and others—to make this faith into which you were baptized more thoroughly *your* own. Become the person who just emerged from the waters—delightfully cleansed and refreshed and renewed in spirit!

For the scripture readings, ask yourself the following:

- Acts of the Apostles 10:34, 37–43—How might I promote the idea of God being for all people?

____

____

____

____

- Colossians 3:1–4—What good may result from my living by what I believe in? Will I try to do this?

____

____

____

____

- John 20:1–9—How can I try to be a "beloved disciple"?

____

____

____

____

For the section on rejecting evil and professing faith (pages 36-43), ask yourself:

- What fears, frights, anxieties, or bonds have I or my parish been freed from? Which ones do I or my parish still need to struggle to overcome?

____

____

____

____

- What can I do to profess my faith in word and action? In other words, how might I continue to affirm my faith in one specific way?

____

____

____

____

- What effect might my baptism have on the way I live each day?

____

____

____

____

As you conclude this first chapter on the mystery of your initiation into Christ's Church, take a moment now to decide what you will do to live what you believe. Of course, you may sometimes feel overwhelmed by life's challenges. However, the committed baptized person makes a contract with Christ—sealing a willingness to face the challenges of life with a renewed heart.

Remember these words of the prophet Ezekiel: "I will give you a new heart and place a new spirit within you" (36:26). In an attitude of faith and trust, recall your conversion to Christ. Respond to the following question now or think about it over the next few days.

- How will I try to free others from what is burdensome to them?

In closing, you may choose to reflect on these words of Cyril of Jerusalem to the newly baptized:

> God, "who has presented you as those who have come alive from the dead," is able to grant to you to "walk in newness of life," because His is the glory and the power, now and forever. Amen.[8]

2

Your New Life of Faith

PSALM–PRAYER

Let the house of Israel say:
    God's love endures forever.
Let the house of Aaron say:
    God's love endures forever.
Let those who fear the LORD say,
    God's love endures forever....

I was hard pressed and falling,
    but the LORD came to my help.
The LORD, my strength and might,
    came to me as savior.

The joyful shout of deliverance
    is heard in the tents of the victors:...

The stone the builders rejected
    has become the cornerstone.
By the LORD has this been done;
    it is wonderful in our eyes.
This is the day the LORD has made;
    let us rejoice in it and be glad.

Psalm 118:2–4, 13–15, 22–24

Overview

This second chapter provides you with the opportunity of looking at your experience of initiation into the Church, specifically with regard to your experience of the ritual of baptism. However, it is not only a review of the liturgy. Rather, it is designed to help you go beyond the events themselves and identify the meaning of baptism for your life today.

You might want to compare this celebration of your initiation to an unfolding drama. You were not a spectator, however; you were part of the celebration and all that came before it.

Discover now what may have been said and done at your baptism. Perhaps what is presented here will help you to go beyond the obvious, to explore what it is you were seeking and became. Continue to engage in conversation, prayer, and reflection with your godparent(s), newly baptized companions, other parishioners, and family members as you journey in faith. Now begin, and continue to uncover your experience of becoming Christian.

EXPLORING YOUR EXPERIENCE

The key symbol of baptism is water. To help you explore the power of water, read the following story. Then try to discover additional aspects of water through the photograph display that follows.

A young man in his mid-twenties stood and breathed in deeply the fresh mountain valley air, moist from several rainfalls that had drenched the valley. It had been sunny and warm earlier in the month, but now dark skies threatened to saturate the valley once again. The month of June had always seemed beautiful before, but this year, as June neared its final week, the skies looked ominous.

The young man, his wife, and their infant son had been visiting the old family home near the river, on their way to a new life in another city. How wonderful it was, after four years away, to return to family and friends in the Wyoming Valley of Pennsylvania. However, they and the many others in the valley were unprepared for what was about to happen. Before dawn on the twenty-third of the month, sirens blared with an uncomfortable roar. They wailed unceasingly. What was going on? Why an air raid drill at this time of the night?

Who would have expected the river to swell to such proportions that not even the enormous dikes could contain the raging river waters? The sirens were signalling a call to evacuate, to move to higher ground. The valley would become a swampland unless the river could be contained.

Many volunteers loaded sandbags to shore up the dikes. Hour after hour the bags were filled and piled high. Workers formed teams, taking breaks more frequently as exhaustion set in. The river, however, would not be denied. A final siren sounded with a shrill beeping tone, warning the volunteers to leave the area as quickly as possible. They were less than three-quarters of a mile from the dike, and it was starting to surrender to the powerful onslaught.

The young man recalls running from the sandbag area. "My family!" he thought. "Where are they? Is this the end?" As he found his family and neighbors, he learned that since their houses were built on a hill, far enough from the river, they would probably be spared the dangerous water. Still, there was much to be done.

For three days, the water rose. Slowly, deliberately, it engulfed the valley. River towns became underwater villages. Some parts of the valley were cut off from neighboring towns, inundated by overflowing creeks. The young couple and their child would eventually seek shelter more than a hundred miles away, with relatives. But for now, the people in the higher elevations had to plan to help those whose homes were slowly succumbing to the raging river.

A supply depot was set up in a service station, about a mile from the river. People pooled their resources, sharing what they had. As food became scarce, an army helicopter landed in the station parking area with bread, milk, and other supplies, enough to last a few more days. Soon after, the water began to subside. It had come within fifty feet of the service station.

People watched and waited as the river slowly receded from the valley's homes. It had demonstrated its awesome power—blanketing the area under twenty feet of water. All that was left was a valley-wide path of mud and debris, with homes shaken from their foundations.

The death toll from this rampaging storm? One person died during the worst stages of the flooding. The victim fell from a boat and drowned while attempting a daring rescue. During this natural disaster, the spunk of the people of this small Pennsylvania valley held up. They worked together to survive and seemingly to say, "Water, we shall absorb your power, tire from your might, but sustain ourselves and go on living with one another's strength." The people of this community rallied around a common purpose, and demonstrated in working together a spirit capable of overcoming even the worst adversity. As one editorial from a local newspaper put it:

> We have weathered the worst that can be inflicted on humans, save a nuclear disaster. We have maintained our courage in the face of bitter tragedy, and we face the future heavily burdened, but secure in the knowledge that help and assistance from many sources is available.
>
> We will rebuild to a better future, supported by our friends here and outside the area, and with faith in our own spirit and with faith in God.[1]

This story tells of the resolve of a community of people to sustain life and to find in some unknown way new life at the end of a dark tunnel of havoc and destruction. Now try to name another example of water's power, preferably from your own life. Describe how the water was a powerful force.

____

____

____

____

Life-Saving Water

The power of water is not only destructive. Water in all its power can be beautiful, serene, and life-saving. Read the following poem, slowly and thoughtfully. Then look at the photographs that follow the poem, and read the poem again.

Water

The sun found the calm spot
facing east, a few minutes
and then it started, drop by
drop winter's frozen mantle
was giving way, and so part
of the ice melted, washing thoughts
away, and at the same time, exposing
others, now being put into focus
by the saving grace of water,
seeking, forever seeking to give
life, a renewal of life, promised
by Jordan's waters, the water will
find its own way, others may share
its saving grace, God-given, salvation.[2]

- What do the poem and photographs tell you about the power and beauty of the symbol of water?

- Why do you think water is the primary symbol in baptism?

Recall your own baptism. Relive standing in the font (or tilting your head) just before the deacon or priest was about to immerse you (or pour water over you).

- As I entered the water, I felt...

  ____

  ____

  ____

  ____

- Did you have a sense of new life as you came out of the water? If you did, what was it? How did it feel?

  ____

  ____

  ____

  ____

Take a walk during the next few days. Quietly observe several ways in which water is used. When you return home, identify some ways you depend on water in your home. As you walk and after you return home, ask yourself: In what way do I take this life-sustaining and life-destroying liquid for granted? In what way do I not?

EXPLORING THE SCRIPTURES

The focus of this chapter is on your experience of baptism—your new life as a Christian. As you read on, think about the image of water presented here. Of all the symbols that could have been chosen, water is the one most closely linked to baptism.

But why would a person seek baptism? Perhaps the phrase "new life" has something to do with why people inquire about becoming Christian. The parish community they begin to identity with may offer a sense of hope and encouragement as they look into becoming Christian. The following remarks may give you a hint of why some newly-baptized people decided to join the Church:

> "I lost the Lord somehow along the way."
>
> "My hopes were just to really learn as much as I could and really have a very strong relationship with God."
>
> "When you walk into that church...I don't know ...I mean, it's definitely the people...even the actual church itself...it's inviting and it's warm....I look at it as a very human type of church."

Note how each of the remarks deals in some way with how people relate to God or to others. Baptism, the sacrament of new life, invites the person to share trust and fellowship with others. These "others"—parishioners—can be a source of friendship and help in good times as well as bad.

- Think back to your baptism. Was there some relationship you wanted to strengthen, that you wanted to give "new life" to?

____

____

____

____

Think, too, of how you relate to others and the impact they may have on your living as a follower of Christ. All of this may help you to reflect on the scriptures that follow and their meaning for your life today.

The Scriptures of the Second Sunday of Easter

The readings for this second Sunday of the Easter season are from the Acts of the Apostles, the first letter of Peter, and the gospel according to John.

Acts of the Apostles 2:42–47

One point of interest in this first reading is how the early Christians changed their ways of living. As you read, try to determine if their way of life is too ideal for you.

The brethren devoted themselves to the apostles' instruction and the communal life, to the breaking of bread and the prayers. A reverent fear overtook them all, for many wonders and signs were performed by the apostles. Those who believed shared all things in common; they would sell their property and goods, dividing everything on the basis of each one's need. They went to the temple area together every day, while in their homes they broke bread. With exultant and sincere hearts they took their meals in common, praising God and winning the approval of all the people. Day by day the Lord added to their number those who were being saved.

The first-century group of believers in Jesus saw their fellowship together as a way of life. The first verse of the passage identifies their activities as four in number: concern for the apostles' teaching; sharing in the communal life in a spirit of fellowship; taking meals together; and sharing prayer. Their religious identity was not something separate from their way of life. It was at the heart of who they were.

A passage such as this one can be very uplifting. It reminds us of how the first disciples of Jesus lived after his resurrection. But in trying to apply its meaning to life today, one may uncover attitudes that need to be guarded against. For example:

> These were the "good old days" of Christianity—it's been downhill ever since!

> These disciples lived in a time that was far less complex than that of today. It was easier for them to sacrifice for one another.

> These people were living around the time of Jesus. They were able to do all those things because they walked in his footsteps.

Attitudes such as these may lead one to question the usefulness of this passage for Jesus' followers today. However, a closer look at the passage may provide some clues for determining its meaning for your life.

These early Christians maintained their temple worship and prayed together in their homes. When they broke bread in their homes, this was not just a coming together to eat at the appointed time. This everyday experience had a religious meaning. Bread is a symbol found throughout the scriptures as a means of maintaining health and life. Bread was used by Jesus to symbolize his remaining union with his disciples. But this is no ordinary symbol. The bread and wine become Jesus' body and blood, to be given to his disciples. The meal-taking of the first Christians may be understood as a sign of the shared love of these believers for the risen Christ—the one whose life they were now invited to share.

- Complete this statement: In my opinion, these believers acted the way they did because...

____

____

____

____

- Some ways one might share with others are by checking with a neighbor who is housebound about his or her need for supplies, assisting in a parish food drive, or encouraging catechumens who are now preparing for baptism. Add a few ways of your own before you continue reading.

____________________ ____________________

____________________ ____________________

____________________ ____________________

1 PETER 1:3–9

The second reading, from Peter's letter to gentile Christians in Asia Minor, explores the new birth given by Jesus Christ. This new birth is "a birth unto hope": what an encouraging statement for the newly baptized! People of hope somehow find something to cling to even in the darkest of circumstances. Whether facing a catastrophic natural disaster, as in the flood story described earlier, or facing a deeply personal sense of loss or aloneness, a spirit of hope can keep one going.

Praised be the God and Father of our Lord Jesus Christ,
he who in his great mercy gave us new birth;
a birth unto hope which draws its life
from the resurrection of Jesus Christ from the dead;
a birth to an imperishable inheritance
incapable of fading or defilement,
which is kept in heaven for you
who are guarded with God's power through faith;
a birth to a salvation which stands ready
to be revealed in the last days.

There is cause for rejoicing here. You may for a time have to suffer the distress of many trials; but this is so that your faith, which is more precious than the passing splendor of fire-tried gold, may by its genuineness lead to praise, glory, and honor when Jesus Christ appears. Although you have never seen him, you love him, and without seeing you believe in him, and rejoice with inexpressible joy touched with glory because you are achieving faith's goal, your salvation.

This passage is from a letter written as encouragement to Christians undergoing suffering at the hands of nonbelieving neighbors in Asia Minor. Peter urges them to "stand fast" for what they believe in and reminds them of the focus of their life of faith—the risen Christ.

In the lengthy first verse of the passage, the writer identifies the many fruits of the new life of Christians. Jesus is the hope for the newly baptized, for those who are suffering and in distress. The reading also addresses the everlasting nature of this new birth, promising "a birth to a salvation which stands ready to be revealed in the last days."

Note the joy that is linked by the writer to a Christian's new birth. An underlying attitude of rejoicing can shape one's whole life, despite the trials and pitfalls one may encounter: trials such as a sudden family illness, loss of a job, lack of purpose in life, lack of communication between parent and child. This does not mean that the Christian is to overlook life's problems, contending that "all that matters is life after death, anyhow." Such an attitude could result in ignoring everyday concerns for which people are struggling to find solutions.

A person is baptized within the community of believers, and not apart from the Church. Christians are challenged to continue to develop an awareness of others' needs and their own responsibility to live justly. You may know people who appear to deny today's problems and their responsibility for helping to solve them. Isolating oneself from life's challenges may result in a private joy that, to an outsider, appears to be no more than selfishness.

The cause for rejoicing in this scripture passage is an attitude of hope that can become for a Christian, like you, a source of "inexpressible joy." An example of such joy is captured in this neophyte's description of a Christian friend: "She can always find that light at the end of the tunnel. When everything's down, she can always find something positive."

Identify one or more areas of your life that may make it difficult for you to live as a person of hope. Perhaps you are facing a "dead end" situation at work, a friendship may be under strain, or you may be at odds with a neighbor.

- How do you feel about this situation? Why is that? What can you do about it?

____

____

____

____

Pray, right now, for the calm and help of the Holy Spirit and those who are close to you to face this situation openly and with a renewed sense of hope. Remember that your parish community is called to be one with you in prayer and in spirit. This is the community that prayed in hope for your ongoing conversion to Christ. Ask others to pray with you if you wish.

JOHN 20:19-31

The gospel for the second Sunday of Easter tells of Jesus' appearance to the disciples after the resurrection. This account includes the widely-known "doubting Thomas" story. There is much to think about in this gospel: for example, what the peace of Jesus can mean; how open Christians are to the Holy Spirit; one's readiness to believe when it is really difficult to do so. You may find a phrase or statement that is especially meaningful to you as you read this passage. Read that part again, more slowly. Then consider why it has special appeal for you.

On the evening of that first day of the week, even though the disciples had locked the doors of the place where they were for fear of the Jews, Jesus came and stood before them. "Peace be with you," he said. When he had said this, he showed them his hands and his side. At the sight of the Lord the disciples rejoiced. "Peace be with you," he said again.

"As the Father has sent me,
so I send you."

Then he breathed on them and said:

"Receive the Holy Spirit.
If you forgive men's sins,
they are forgiven them;
if you hold them bound,
they are held bound."

It happened that one of the Twelve, Thomas (the name means "Twin"), was absent when Jesus came. The other disciples kept telling him: "We have seen the Lord!" His answer was, "I'll never believe it without probing the nail-prints in his hands, without putting my finger in the nail-marks and my hand into his side."

A week later, the disciples were once more in the room, and this time Thomas was with them. Despite the locked doors, Jesus came and stood before them. "Peace be with you," he said; then, to Thomas: "Take your finger and examine my hands. Put your hand into my side. Do not persist in your unbelief, but believe!" Thomas said in response, "My Lord and my God!" Jesus then said to him:

"You became a believer because you saw me.
Blest are they who have not seen and have believed."

Jesus performed many other signs as well—signs not recorded here—in the presence of his disciples. But these have been recorded to help you believe that Jesus is the Messiah, the Son of God, so that through this faith you may have life in his name.

The disciples of Jesus are huddled together on the evening of Easter, fearful after Jesus' death on the cross. Jesus comes to them, however, offers them peace, and then offers it again. This peace is no ordinary greeting—a first-century substitute for "Hello, there." Rather it is an expression of what Jesus himself brings to his disciples: loving concern, calm, lack of fear... in a word, peace.

One is reminded of Jesus' words to his disciples before he died: "I have told you this so that you might have peace in me. In the world you will have trouble, but take courage, I have conquered the world" (John 16:33). Indeed, it appears that Jesus is preparing his disciples for the mission he gives them. He breathes on them and offers the gift of his Spirit and power to forgive sin. The breathing of Jesus is no accident—he could have just as easily used words alone or even presumed the disciples' willingness to do as he asked. In the word "breathe," one may really see echoes of the creation of humanity in Genesis 2:7: "The Lord God formed man out of the clay of the ground and blew into his nostrils the breath of life, and so man became a living being."

Jesus' gift to his disciples is the gift of new life, the gift which is yours, too, in baptism. Jesus' gift is the Holy Spirit, the Easter gift of the risen Lord. Become more aware now of the refreshing breath of life that is yours. Sit in a comfortable chair, and let all your muscles relax. Feel the relaxation from head to toe. Now take a deep breath, all the way in. Slowly exhale. Then repeat the breathing exercise. Know that the Spirit of God is deep within your heart. Jot down how you feel in the space below.

____

____

____

____

The gospel passage goes on to describe the absence of Thomas the apostle from the appearance of Jesus on Easter night. One really has to feel sympathy for Thomas. In a way he represents the doubt of all of the disciples regarding Jesus' resurrection. But, as the passage of time and the concreteness of history would have it, only Thomas is named as doubting the Easter event. Poor Thomas!

Thomas' attitude is one of unbelief until it can be proven to him that Jesus is truly risen. He refuses to accept even the evidence offered by his friends ("We have seen the Lord!"). He persists in his attitude of wanting only to see for himself, as if to say, "Hey, I want to see this miracle, too!" How sad for Thomas that he would not—or could not—trust his friends. But what a turnaround occurs when he casts his eyes on Jesus! Without even touching the risen one, Thomas firmly declares, "My Lord and my God!"

The last part of the passage shows the purpose of John's gospel: to help believers deepen their faith in Jesus as the Messiah and Son of God. Through faith in Jesus, the believer is called to new life. The source of this new life is Jesus himself. What is necessary is not seeing, but believing in Jesus as the Christ, the Son of God.

- What role do you think "hearing" plays in faith?

- What role do you think "seeing" plays in faith?

- How do you feel about trusting the word of others when it is "hearsay"?

- Is it sometimes difficult for you to place your trust in God? Why is that?

To further explore doubt and trust in your life, choose one of the following phrases and discuss with a friend or spouse what you could do to make the phrase into a statement of trust. For example, you may want to complete the line "I'm not sure about . . ." with the phrase "what I believe sometimes. I get confused, but have a close friend who helps me sort things out." Complete the sentence and redirect it so that an attitude of trust starts to emerge.

Sample phrases:

"I'm not sure about. . . ."

"I just don't know if. . . ."

"That's ridiculous! How naive can you get? I just can't. . . ."

"If I could only find this one last thing out, then I'd be willing to. . . ."

RENEWING YOUR LIFE OF FAITH

In preparing to join the Church, one word may have been repeated often to describe the gift of new life: baptism. Although you may sometimes think of baptism as a specific moment in time, for example, "when I was baptized," it is part of initiation into the Church. Perhaps one could describe it as a journey over time to saying "yes" to a lifestyle founded on the life of Christ.

All during the catechumenate you may have experienced:

- a sense of rebirth in your own life;
- the prayer of others with you and for you;
- the help and hope of your sponsor (or godparent, if not the same person) and parish Church community.

Your entry into the faith of the church was probably a gradual experience, as you began to explore what it meant to believe and to live as a Christian. You may have discovered how much you relied on others to help you identify what you believed and what choices were before you. Then, at a particular moment in time or gradually over time, you may have decided to continue your journey of faith by agreeing to stand before your parish and enter the waters of new life.

In its own way, your parish probably supported your willingness to become a Christian by acknowledging your commitment to a Christian way of life. Your immediate preparation for baptism resulted in your immersion in the water of new birth. In the early church, it was customary for people to be baptized by immersion. Later on, pouring of water over the candidate, who was standing in a pool, became a popular practice. Today, baptismal practice varies within Christianity. Discover more now of what the celebration of baptism meant for you.

Think back now to your baptism. Look at the photograph of the rolling ocean waves on the next page. Imagine your passage through the waters of new birth. You entered into the paschal mystery of Christ by sharing in his death and resurrection. You may have felt like a "new creation" in the midst of your parish Church community.

The Liturgy of Baptism

The water used for your baptism was blessed as part of the celebration of the sacrament. This "blessing declares the religious meaning of water as God's creation and the sacramental use of water in the unfolding of the paschal mystery, and the blessing is also a remembrance of God's wonderful works in the history of salvation" (*RCIA*, #210).[3]

The sacramental symbol of water is also addressed in this blessing. The presider prays that the power of the Spirit will give the grace of Jesus to the waters being blessed.

If you were baptized at the Easter Vigil, the priest would have lowered the Easter candle into the font or pool of water as he said this concluding part of the prayer of blessing:

> We ask you, Father, with your Son
> to send the Holy Spirit upon the waters of this font.
> May all who are buried with Christ in the death of
> baptism
> rise also with him to newness of life.
>
> We ask this through Christ our Lord (*RCIA*, #222).[4]

Into the Water

Do you remember the touch of the celebrant and your godparent(s) as the celebrant immersed you in the water (or poured water over you) three times, and brought you up out of the water? The celebrant said:

> N., I baptize you in the name of the Father,
> and of the Son,
> and of the Holy Spirit (*RCIA*, #226).[5]

You were baptized!

One newly baptized person, after being asked what she remembered from her baptism, remarked:

> Getting water dumped on me! And this whole congregation looking at me...and I thought "O, my God"...and cheering....I remember everything. ...it was so exciting.

- Complete this statement: When I was immersed or felt the water being poured on me, I...

____

____

____

____

The Completion of Baptism

The celebration of confirmation—of the sealing of your baptism with the gift of the Holy Spirit—came just before the liturgy of the eucharist. Confirmation is the completion of your baptism. Their joint celebration shows "the unity of the paschal mystery, the close link between the mission of the Son and the outpouring of the Holy Spirit, and the connection between the two sacraments through which the Son and the Holy Spirit come with the Father to those who are baptized" (*RCIA*, #215).[6]

Search your inner self for the promptings of the Spirit in your life. Be alive in the Spirit of the risen Lord! "The love of God has been poured out into our hearts through the holy Spirit that has been given to us" (Romans 5:5).

Up from the Water

Your baptism was one in a long line of baptismal celebrations over the ages. Christian baptism is rooted in the scriptures and is part of a long tradition. As you saw in chapter 1 the fathers of the Church, speaking in the fourth century, explored the baptism celebration with the newly baptized in descriptive and symbolic language. Perhaps what some of these fathers said then can help you now as you reflect on the meaning of your own initiation into the Church.

Two basic themes dominate the fathers' preaching on baptism: union with Christ in his death and resurrection and the whole idea of new birth, or new life in Christ.[7] Theodore of Mopsuestia compared the water to a womb that protects the person who is being baptized. Just as the conceived child has lived in the shelter and security of its mother's womb, so, too, does the candidate for baptism experience, in a symbolic way, the womb-like protection of the water. The newly baptized emerges from the water-like womb born anew to live as a Christian. Theodore told his listeners:

> You descend into the water, which has been consecrated by the benediction of the priest, as you are not baptised only with ordinary water, but with the water of the second birth, which cannot become so except through the coming of the Holy Spirit (on it). For this it is necessary that the priest should have beforehand made use of clear words, according to the rite of the priestly service, and asked God that the grace of the Holy Spirit might come on the water and impart to it the power both of conceiving that awe-inspiring child and becoming a womb to the sacramental birth.[8]

The symbols mentioned above, and in the remaining parts of this book, are important, of course. They can help you uncover the meaning of your baptism. However, it is most important that you not lose sight of the one toward which all the symbols point: Jesus Christ. Water, candle, robe, light, and so on—all have their place. But when all the symbols are stripped away, Jesus is the one who remains, saying simply, in effect, "Come! Follow me."

John Chrysostom was a priest at Antioch during the fourth century. Try to go beneath the symbols as you read these remarks of Chrysostom, delivered to those seeking and awaiting baptism:

> The priest makes you go down into the sacred waters, burying the old man and at the same time raising up the new, who is renewed in the image of his Creator. It is at this moment that, through the words and the hand of the priest, the Holy Spirit descends upon you. Instead of the man who descended into the water, a different man comes forth, one who has wiped away all the filth of his sins, who has put off the old garment of sin and has put on the royal robe....
>
> When the priest says: "So-and-so is baptized in the name of the Father, and of the Son, and of the Holy Spirit," he puts your head down into the water three times and three times he lifts it up again, preparing you by this mystic rite to receive the descent of the Spirit.[9]

John Chrysostom did not intend his words to be taken just as an instruction on the liturgy of baptism. His preaching was intended to help his listeners in their everyday lives. Chrysostom's purpose was to move the hearts of his hearers, to motivate them to act as persons who had chosen to live the way of Christ:

> As you come forth from the waters, symbolizing your resurrection by rising up from them, ask Him to be your ally, so that you may guard well the gifts He has given you, and that you may not be conquered by the deceits of the wicked one. Beg Him for peace among the churches, beseech Him for those who are being led astray, prostrate yourselves in

behalf of those who are in sin, so that we may be judged worthy of mercy in some degree. For He has granted you great confidence, He has enrolled you in the front ranks of His friends, and has received into the adoption of sons you who were formerly captives and slaves with no right to speak out. He will not reject your prayers; again imitating in this His own goodness, He will grant you everything you ask.[10]

Chrysostom's words parallel themes of baptism you may have already heard: union with Christ, sharing in his death and resurrection, the presence of the Holy Spirit in your life. After all your preparation for baptism, these points may appear to be no more than what your preparation was leading you to: the pouring of the water. Imagine, however, these ideas as points of departure for your life. Perhaps all during your preparation for baptism you were considering how you relate to Christ and were responding to the Spirit of God in your life. You might want to think again about what meaning this has for your life now and for the future. One or more of the following situations may help you to do this.

- One newly baptized person, speaking of her relationship with her husband, said: "In him I see Christ a lot...it's always 'calm down, take a deep breath, don't worry about it!'" How does the way you relate to Christ affect the way you relate to others? Why is that?

____

____

____

____

- City planners decide to replace an unattractive downtown urban neighborhood with a futuristic mall designed to include exclusive boutiques and high-priced apartments. The decision will result in displacing hundreds of low-income families. Where do you stand on this situation? What might a parish do to help local residents? What could "resurrection" mean to them?

____

____

____

____

- The spirit and determination of the aging Japanese grandfather could not be moved. For years he had carried within him pictures and images of the horror he witnessed in Hiroshima. But how could he help others learn from this terrible event? Now, years later, an artist listened intently to the old man's description of the Hiroshima bombing. His lips quivering, his eyes reddened, swollen, and tear-filled, the old man described what he had seen on August 6, 1945. Slowly, the lines of the artist began to give shape to the old man's memories, no longer bottled up inside himself. Pause here for a moment. Then compare the determination of the Japanese grandfather to your own. Complete this statement: The thing that keeps me going when I make up my mind to do something is.... This is because....

____

____

____

____

Did You Know?

The white garment that your godparent(s) may have placed on you after your baptism was a further sign of the meaning of what had just occurred. The celebrant told you that you had become a new creation, clothing yourself with Christ. Paul writes in his letter to the Galatians: "For all of you who were baptized into Christ have clothed yourselves with Christ" (3:27).

One may benefit today from early baptismal practices, even though extensive first-hand information may not be available. For the Church fathers of the fourth century, the baptismal garment had several meanings. Among these were union with the risen Christ, living a life faithful to Christ, and forgiveness of sin. For example, John Chrysostom often spoke of "putting on Christ," citing the verse from Paul given above. He urged his listeners to keep the garment clean, so that they would be able to share in the eternal life to come. Chrysostom also told his hearers:

> Did you see the power of this garment? Did you see the luster of this robe which time cannot touch, which age cannot dim? Did you see its irresistible beauty? . . .
>
> Prayer, above all, can guard continuously for us the luster of this spiritual garment. Along with prayer goes generosity in almsgiving, which is our crowning good deed and the means of our soul's salvation.[11]

One newly baptized person has made this observation about the symbols of baptism:

> All that was still new to me . . . symbols and all that stuff. . . . I didn't understand them at the time . . . it just was like, frightening . . . baptism . . . that was great . . . the big white robe you had to wear. . . . It was gigantic!

- Think back to the time when you wore your baptismal robe. What did it mean to you then? What does it mean to you now?

  ___

  ___

  ___

  ___

ACCEPTING THE CHALLENGE

The story of your initiation into the Church does not occur in isolation from other Christians. Members of your parish may have helped you work through questions you had or doubts you experienced about becoming a Christian. Your sponsor and parishioners you have come to know and respect may have shown by the "lesson of their lives" what it is to live in an attitude of faith shaped by belief in Jesus Christ. Now, as you approach the conclusion of this chapter, explore further what it can mean for you to accept the challenge of your baptism.

New Life, Daily Life

What is the challenge of your "new life"? You may hear homilies on living as a committed Christian, as a person baptized in water and the Spirit. Yet this new life is not intended to separate you from problems you may have. Rather, it is intended to be a source of strength to help you live each day in a spirit of trust and hope. You can become a "realistic optimist"—looking forward to the fullness of life with God while at the same time trying to cope with the tensions of life today. Read, for example, the following:

> There's plenty of water where I live. No need to worry about a drought. I just can't believe that the world, which is mostly water, could have such problems. It's probably all made up by politicians anyway.

This statement suggests that a water problem does not exist unless one is affected personally. A closer look, however, might show that one need not be directly affected to be personally involved. Water is a vital resource for all of life, and not just for "my life." Water, indeed, is necessary for salvation! People must ask themselves if they see this water as a resource for life or a commodity to be absorbed and even wasted. Do you feel the need to be better informed about water–related issues? Why or why not?

____

____

____

____

Looking Back

Review briefly some of the highlights of the sections on the scriptures (pages 56-66) and renewing your life of faith (pages 66-75). As you may have done in chapter 1, consider what has challenged you or what you wish to move beyond. Try to refine what your baptism in water and the Spirit means for your life now, in a practical sort of way.

The questions that follow may help you to focus on your attitude as a Christian. They may challenge you to rethink decisions you have made or judgments you have formed.

For the scripture readings, ask yourself the following questions.

- Acts of the Apostles 2:42–47—What responsibility do I have toward making newcomers feel welcome in my parish, neighborhood, or town? Will I?

  ____

  ____

  ____

  ____

- 1 Peter 1:3–9—How do I project myself and my attitude to others?

  ____

  ____

  ____

  ____

- John 20:19–31—Should I work on or change any of my attitudes toward others because of the way I have judged a situation or another person? Will I?

  ____

  ____

  ____

  ____

For the section on exploring the meaning of baptism (pages 66-75), begin by reading the following poem.

Baptism

Water, flowing quickly
Streams of wonder I behold.
Yet how gently strength arises
And gives to me a hundredfold.

O, these fountains of joy unending
O, these brooks of lasting peace!
Silent, flowing, gently easing,
Carve into my life, appeasing.

Winds its way through many caverns
Bubbling, churning,
Filling, swelling,
Wonderful, compelling.

Cool and clear, I drink with delight
For the rays of day break forth
How I feel how much I'm loving
All the joys of my new birth.[12]

- A line in this poem that appeals to me is . . . because. . . My most vivid memory of my baptism is . . .

____

____

____

____

- In your opinion, what are the most significant points of the section on renewing your life of faith (pages 66-75)? How do you think they will influence you? What will you do the same? Differently?

____

____

____

____

LIGHT THE DARKNESS

As you conclude this chapter on your initiation as a Christian, take into your hands your baptism candle. Perhaps you can gather with others for this moment of prayer. Feel the smooth texture of the wax and look at the symbols impressed on the candle.

At your baptism, a godparent handed you a lighted candle after you were draped and fitted with the baptismal robe. It was lighted from the Easter candle and signified your sharing in the life of Christ who is our light. Jesus said, "I am the light of the world. Whoever follows me will not walk in darkness, but will have the light of life" (John 8:12).

Light the candle. Focus on the symbols that identify Jesus Christ as the beginning (A) and the end (Ω), and that indicate the first two letters of the sacred name Christ in Greek (X and P). Notice, too, the symbol of the dove—a symbol of the peace and gift of the Spirit that is yours.

Put the candle on a table or countertop in front of you. Watch it burn. Then read slowly these words from the liturgy of baptism:

You have been enlightened by Christ. [Pick up candle.]
Walk always as children of the light. [Move candle from left to right.]
and keep the flame of faith alive in your hearts. [Look directly at the flame.]
When the Lord comes, may you go out to meet him
with all the saints in the heavenly kingdom.

[Pause for a few seconds, then extinguish the candle.] (*RCIA*, #230)[13]

3

The Center of Your Life of Faith

PSALM–PRAYER

Keep me safe, O God;
    in you I take refuge.
I say to the LORD,
    you are my LORD,
    you are my only good. . . .
LORD, my allotted portion and my cup,
    you have made my destiny secure. . . .

I bless the LORD who counsels me;
    even at night my heart exhorts me.
I keep the LORD always before me;
    with the LORD at my right, I shall never be shaken.
Therefore my heart is glad, my soul rejoices;
    my body also dwells secure,
For you will not abandon me to Sheol,
    nor let your faithful servant see the pit.
You will show me the path to life,
    abounding joy in your presence,
    the delights at your right hand forever.

Psalm 16:1–2, 5, 7–11

Overview

What a liturgy, this Easter Vigil! In the atmosphere of a dark evening, made shining with the light of Christ, you were baptized and celebrated the eucharist for the first time. The events of that night may have even overwhelmed you.

In this chapter you are invited to explore the meaning of the eucharist for your life. Many words have been used to try to capture the meaning of the eucharist. One word seems very appropriate here, however. That is the word "center." Now that you are a neophyte, the eucharist can become the center of your life of faith.

As with previous chapters, there are various activities that may help you to explore the theme of the chapter. Continue now your journey of faith. Join with others if at all possible. May your hunger for eucharist never end!

EXPLORING YOUR EXPERIENCE

In chapter 1 you read: "By discovering what it means to live as a Christian in the world one may be able to begin to live out the consequences of the resurrection. In rising from death, Jesus provides a hope for meeting the challenges that confront people and that can prevent them from becoming their best selves."

For a baptized person, like you, the eucharist can become the center of your hope. The eucharist can become not only what Christians hunger for themselves, but what they yearn to share with others. When you see a need in someone else's life and try to help, then you are living the eucharist. When you take a stand and voice your concern about an important issue, then you are living the eucharist. What it boils down to is this: the way you choose to live as a Christian should be, for you, one example of your faith in Jesus' presence in your life.

Catechumens may experience Jesus' presence in their lives through the help of a sponsor, the reading of the scriptures, or the expressions of support they experience when with other catechumens.

- Recall your journey as a catechumen. Then complete this statement: One example of Jesus' presence in my life while I was a catechumen is...

  ___

  ___

  ___

  ___

If you were baptized at the Easter Vigil, the liturgy did not conclude with the baptism or anointing with chrism that followed. How incomplete it would have been if the assembly had left then. Can you imagine what it would have been like if, after a resounding acknowledgment of welcome, perhaps with applause, the church would have emptied? No, there was more to be done, more to be celebrated.

On this night of the vigil, you shared for the first time in the sacrament of the eucharist. Paul wrote to the Corinthians: "Because the loaf of bread is one, we, though many, are one body, for we all partake of the one loaf" (1 Corinthians 10:17). You were fully initiated now, ready to take your place alongside the already baptized. You were to eat with them weekly, to offer with them the gifts of bread and wine to the Father of all. Your whole journey as a catechumen was leading you to this "center of the whole Christian life" (*RCIA*, #243).[1] You had come to the altar of new life, ready to share in the eucharist.

Coming to the Altar

The image of coming to the altar was used frequently by Ambrose, the bishop of Milan, in his sermons to the newly baptized toward the end of the fourth century. On three different days of Easter week, neophytes would hear Ambrose remind them: "You have come to the altar." His words may now be directed to you, for you, too, have come to the altar.

There follows your coming to the altar. You began to come; the angels observed; they saw you approaching, and that human condition which before was stained with the shadowy squalor of sins they saw suddenly shining bright, and so they said: "Who is this that cometh up from the desert whitewashed?" So the angels also marvel. Do you wish to know how they marvel? Hear the Apostle Peter saying that those things have been conferred on you which the angels also desired to see. Hear again. It says: "The eye hath not seen, nor ear heard what things God hath prepared for them that love him...."

You have come, then, to the altar; you have received the grace of Christ; you have obtained the heavenly sacraments. The Church rejoices in the redemption of many, and is glad with spiritual exultation that the members of her household are at hand dressed in white. You have this in the Canticle of Canticles. Rejoicing, she invokes Christ, having prepared a banquet, which seems worthy of heavenly feasting.[2]

Ambrose's words are full of imagery for the newly baptized: angels, the desert, being dressed in white. His imaginative style enables him to describe the wonder of the neophytes' first sharing in the eucharist. For Ambrose, all of creation is made new in the death and resurrection of Jesus. Ambrose's style might win for him today the title of the "Bishop with the Power of Heavenly Promise."

Today Christians might see their coming to the altar in a different way. Slowly read the following poem. Then complete the statements that follow.

The Offering

The offering, of one plus one plus one
    on and on and on
Adding up to more than all of us
Slowly we approach the table
Gathering 'round this bread, this cup
Bless you, Lord,
    for all your creation!

Bless you, Lord,
    for these fruits of our hands!
We present ourselves to you,
    our lives the gifts we share
We place ourselves before you
    sealed in space and time
Where all before meets all that is after
Where all that is under
    soars beyond all heights
Simple gifts
    our bread, our wine
    blessed, broken
Nourishment
    for the journey from the water
Hope for the unknown day
    breaking forth
    in the freedom of the Spirit
Bonding us, empowering us
God within us
A prayer of life
    and a common sacrifice
    of love poured out
    faith transformed
    hunger satisfied
    thirst quenched
    God among us
    renewing our strength
    to witness in love
    and to come to the altar
    another day.

- A line from the poem that appeals to me is ______________________________

  ____

  I chose this line because ____

  ____

- Recall a time in your life without eucharist. Now complete the following.

  For me, the eucharist is ______________________________

  ____

  This is because ______________________________

  ____

EXPLORING THE SCRIPTURES

The focus of this chapter is your experience of the eucharist and your sharing in and going from this sacred meal and sacrifice to serve others.

You may have prepared for eucharist for a long time as part of your conversion to Christ and initiation into the Church. Your conversion may have been gradual, slowly winding its way over the rough and smooth edges of your life. Along the way you may have felt:

- the joy of new relationships with others;
- trust that your sponsor would be with you;
- doubt about what you were doing;
- a warm embrace when words would not do;
- loneliness when you felt misunderstood;
- a burning love for Jesus;
- sadness when someone left the group;
- the Spirit speaking in your heart;
- a wonderful new experience of hospitality;
- disillusionment with something you were told.

The way you felt as you prepared for baptism may help you to reflect on what your sharing in the eucharist, the Bread of Life, means to you as food for your faith journey. Perhaps this will lead you to explore what you and your parish are called to be for others and to do now on behalf of others. It may also help you to prepare to read the scriptures that follow.

The Scriptures of the Third Sunday of Easter

The readings for this third Sunday of the Easter season are from the Acts of the Apostles, the first letter of Peter, and the gospel according to Luke.

ACTS OF THE APOSTLES 2:14, 22–28

In this reading, Peter boldly announces what was to become the core belief of Christianity: that God freed Jesus from death and raised him up. As you read, reflect on dying and rising in your life, and how this is all part of what it means for you as a Christian.

[On the day of Pentecost] Peter stood up with the Eleven, raised his voice, and addressed them: "You who are Jews, indeed all of you staying in Jerusalem! Listen to what I have to say: Men of Israel, listen to me! Jesus the Nazorean was a man whom God sent to you with miracles, wonders and signs as his credentials. These God worked through him in your midst, as you well know. He was delivered up by the set purpose and plan of God; you even used pagans to crucify and kill him. God freed him from death's bitter pangs, however, and raised him up again, for it was impossible that death should keep its hold on him. David says of him:

'I have set the Lord ever before me,
with him at my right hand I shall not be disturbed.
My heart has been glad and my tongue has rejoiced,
my body will live on in hope,
For you will not abandon my soul to the nether world,
nor will you suffer your faithful one to undergo corruption.
You have shown me the paths of life;
you will fill me with joy in your presence.'"

In chapter 1 of this book, you read Peter's last great discourse. This one is his first. The scene for this passage is Pentecost Sunday. The disciples were gathered together in Jerusalem and had just been "filled with the holy Spirit" (Acts 2:4). They boldly began to speak of "the mighty acts of God" (Acts 2:11). Accused by some of speaking like drunkards, Peter rises and begins the sermon recorded above. One can still imagine the fiery and compulsive Peter jumping to his feet! He tries to show that Jesus was the Promised One, the Messiah. The cross could not hold Jesus captive: "it was impossible that death should keep its hold on him."

Consider the dyings and risings people go through today. Perhaps someone you know has suffered a serious setback in business, while another has just healed a broken friendship. A mother may gaze lovingly at a photograph of her missing child on a milk carton, wondering if they will ever be united again. A teenager may overcome drug dependency after a struggle that at one time had seemed futile.

The deaths people experience today may not steal a last breath, but may provide a clue as to what must be done to overcome evil and injustice. For example, one may be poorly informed or misinformed about the AIDS epidemic that has gripped society. A person may be tempted to make snap judgments based on sketchy news reports or slick ad campaigns. In resisting such judgments people begin to overcome evil that might otherwise overtake them.

- Complete the chart that follows. Identify in the first column situations of dying in your own life, your parish, and the nation. Then tell in the second column what you, your parish, and the nation might do to rise against these dyings.

Dyings and Risings of Life

	Dying	*Rising*
Your Life	______	______
	______	______
Your Parish	______	______
	______	______
Your Nation	______	______
	______	______

The passage from Acts on page 87 concludes with Peter quoting a Psalm of David (Psalm 16:8–11). Reread this part of the passage ("David says of him…"). Then ask yourself:

- What might I do today to help another person "live on in hope"?

______

______

______

______

1 PETER 1:17–21

This passage is very brief—only five verses long. But you may want to read it more than once. Peter does not beg or meekly ask the baptized to believe what he says. In this and surrounding passages, he urges the baptized to remain faithful to God, for they are made new by Christ.

In prayer you call upon a Father who judges each one justly, on the basis of his actions. Since this is so, conduct yourselves reverently during your sojourn in a strange land. Realize that you were delivered from the futile way of life your fathers handed on to you, not by any diminishable sum of silver or gold but by Christ's blood beyond all price: the blood of a spotless, unblemished lamb chosen before the world's foundation and revealed for your sake in these last days. It is through him you are believers in God, the God who raised him from the dead and gave him glory. Your faith and hope, then, are centered in God.

Peter reminds the baptized that they are delivered "by Christ's blood beyond all price." Indeed, Jesus sacrificed himself for all. He surrendered, sacrificed, yielded all for all humanity. This blood image is a very powerful one. The blood of the lamb was sprinkled on the lintel and doorposts of the homes of the Israelites to protect them from being struck down as the Egyptians were (Exodus 12:21–30). In Israelite law, the use of blood, symbolic of life itself, was particularly important in sacrificial rites of forgiveness (Leviticus 17:1–16). Moses, in ratifying the Sinai covenant, splashed blood on the altar and sprinkled it on the people, saying, "This is the blood of the covenant which the Lord has made with you in accordance with all these words of his" (Exodus 24:8). And during the Passover meal, Jesus took a cup of wine, gave thanks, and passed it to his disciples. "He said to them: 'This is my blood of the covenant, which will be shed for many'" (Mark 14:24).

What else might one learn about this blood symbol? One writer, Ralph Keifer, in writing about "the body/blood phraseology" of the New Testament, notes:

> The form of Christ's death was crucifixion, a basically bloodless death by suffocation. The body/blood language [of the New Testament] refers not to the form of Christ's death, but to its *meaning*, as the event bringing God and humankind together in reconciliation.... Christ is the one who reconciles us to the Father, and to share in the eucharistic meal is to share in that reconciliation.... To share in the eucharistic meal is to share in the sacrificial event of Christ's death.[3]

What may be important to a Christian, like you, is how Jesus' death and resurrection relate to your faith in Christ and to how you live your life today. Surely, Peter did not intend to provide only an explanation of past events. His purpose was to move his readers to action, to see those events as somehow present in their own lives.

A Christian is joined to Christ in the food of the eucharist, and shares in Jesus' dying and rising. Christians are called not only to share this food, but also to share themselves as people nourished by Christ. Baptized people, then, do not only recall God's saving action in the past. They ask the Father to be with them, enabling them to live as people strengthened by Christ in the eucharist.

What else might one want to explore about this life-saving and supreme-surrendering gift of Jesus to us? The *RCIA* notes your new standing in the community this way. Notice how clearly you are now joined to the community of faith in becoming one in the eucharist and sharers of Christ's body and blood:

> With the entire community they share in the offering of the sacrifice and say the Lord's Prayer, giving expression to the spirit of adoption as God's children that they have received in baptism. When in communion they receive the body that was given for us and the blood that was shed, the neophytes are strengthened in the gifts they have already received and are given a foretaste of the eternal banquet (*RCIA*, #217).[4]

Your hunger for the eternal banquet is not a singular one. Such hunger pains are not limited only to each person individually. Rather, we hunger as a community of faith, sharing in the body and blood of the risen one, surrendering our lives to him and one another as we await the eternal banquet of life everlasting.

- Look around your neighborhood or town. What evidence is there of Christians living by what they believe?

___

___

___

___

- The year is 2096. Something you did in 1996, and that you thought was quite ordinary, has had lasting impact on scores of people for a century. Complete this statement: One thing I might have done that would have had such an impact is...

___

___

___

___

This is because...

___

___

___

___

LUKE 24:13-35

Read slowly, twice, the following excerpt from a poem by Walt Whitman.

Song of the Open Road
(an excerpt)

Allons! the road is before us!
It is safe—I have tried it—my own feet have
 tried it well—be not detain'd! . . .

Camerado, I give you my hand!
I give you my love more precious than money,
I give you myself before preaching or law;
Will you give me yourself? will you come travel
 with me?
Shall we stick by each other as long as we live?[5]

- Recall a memorable journey you have made. Were you alone? With a companion? Why did you go?

____

____

____

____

Now read the passage that follows.

Two disciples of Jesus that same day [the first day of the sabbath] were making their way to a village named Emmaus seven miles distant from Jerusalem, discussing as they went all that had happened. In the course of their lively exchange, Jesus approached and began to walk along with them. However, they were restrained from recognizing him. He said to them, "What are you discussing as you go your way?" They halted in distress, and one of them, Cleopas by name, asked him, "Are you the only resident of Jerusalem who does not know the things that went on there these past few days?" He said to them, "What things?" They said: "All those that had to do with Jesus of Nazareth, a prophet powerful in word and deed in the eyes of God and all the people; how our chief priests and leaders delivered him up to be condemned to death, and crucified him. We were hoping that he was the one who would set Israel free. Besides all this, today, the third day since these things happened, some women of our group have just brought us some astonishing news. They were at the tomb before dawn and failed to find his body, but returned with the tale that they had seen a vision of angels who declared he was alive. Some of our number went to the tomb and found it just as the women said; but him they did not see."

Then he said to them, "What little sense you have! How slow you are to believe all that the prophets have announced! Did not the Messiah have to undergo all this so as to enter into his glory?" Beginning, then, with Moses and all the prophets, he interpreted for them every passage of Scripture which referred to him. By now they were near the village to which they were going, and he acted as if he were going farther. But they pressed him: "Stay with us. It is nearly evening—the day is practically over." So he went in to stay with them.

When he had seated himself with them to eat, he took bread, pronounced the blessing, then broke the bread and began to distribute it to them. With that their eyes were opened and they recognized him; whereupon he vanished from their sight. They said to one another, "Were not our hearts burning inside us as he talked to us on the road and explained the Scriptures to us?" They got up immediately and returned to Jerusalem, where they found the Eleven and the rest of the company assembled. They were greeted with, "The Lord has been raised! It is true! He has appeared to Simon." Then they recounted what had happened on the road and how they had come to know him in the breaking of bread.

What a walk! Seven miles—a long journey by foot. Perhaps it will help to retell some highlights of the story here. The travelers, two disciples of Jesus who had hoped he was the Messiah, are ready to go home from Jerusalem. After being there for the events surrounding the Passover and Jesus' death, they set out, discussing as they go all that had happened during the last few days. An inquiring stranger comes by and joins them. The trio walk and talk for hours. This leads the two who had begun the journey to wonder about their mysterious companion. Perhaps they thought, "He knows so much about the scriptures, yet he does not know what happened in Jerusalem?"

The wonder of the travelers does not lead them to part from the stranger; rather, their curiosity and puzzlement move them to invite him to stay with them. Before long, they are sharing a meal. Though it is not his home, the stranger plays host, serving the two travelers bread blessed and broken. In the breaking of bread, their eyes are opened, and the traveler-host vanishes. However, they feel no absence. Strange, isn't it? In the absence of the stranger they are conscious of the presence of the Messiah. Nourished by the word of God on their way to Emmaus, the travelers share the bread that was broken and given to them by the one whose presence they had hungered for. Despite the growing darkness, they hurry back to Jerusalem and tell the story of how they had come to know the stranger in the breaking of the bread.

There are interesting parallels to the celebration of the eucharist here. Jesus explains the scriptures to the two disciples, and the action of sharing the bread resembles what Jesus did at the Passover meal: "Then he took the bread, said the blessing, broke it, and gave it to them" (Luke 22:19). One might imagine how Jesus, as a faithful Jew, would gather annually with other Jews to recall the great Exodus experience of Passover. Perhaps their feelings were of entering into the Passover event itself—of somehow knowing a freedom from bondage that could not be duplicated. It is from within this sacred setting—that of a meal—that Jesus came to us under the appearances of bread and wine.

What you may want to take from this first resurrection account of Luke's gospel, though, is more than an awareness of scriptural comparisons. You have a story to tell, just as the travelers did who risked the return trip to Jerusalem.

The challenge for a Christian may be to share Jesus' presence with others, as he shares his presence with you. This means more than presenting oneself on Sunday to "hear mass." It means:

- becoming aware of the eucharist as a sacrament of Christians united in the Spirit as the body of Christ, with Christians working together as a Church called to carry on the work of Christ;
- taking a close look at what you value, and clarifying for yourself how Jesus is the center of your life of faith;
- exploring how Jesus makes a difference in your attitudes and in how you relate to people who are close to you—and those who are not.

The travelers in the story did not recognize the stranger on the way to Emmaus. Was there a time recently when you did not see what was right before you; when you couldn't see the forest for the trees? What did you do?

____

____

____

____

Sometimes it is easier to avoid an issue than to face it, to close rather than open one's eyes. In the chart that follows, identify two of your favorite "I don't want to talk about it" issues. Ask yourself why you avoid the issue. Conclude by suggesting first steps to overcome your fear.

Avoidance Issues

Issues I Avoid	*Why I Avoid Them*	*Overcoming My Fear*

You may decide to seek support from other people if you choose to try to overcome your fear. Your confidence in their ability to help is an important step toward facing difficult and controversial issues openly. Make your own the words of Ambrose of Milan:

> Open your ears and enjoy the good odor of eternal life which has been breathed upon you by the grace of the sacraments.[6]

RENEWING YOUR LIFE OF FAITH

The celebration of eucharist is a wonderful invitation for a baptized person, like you, to renew one's faith. You may affirm what you believe in the profession of faith. You may discover anew the power of the Spirit of God in gathering with others, in the prayer of the faithful, and in the actions of people and priest-presider. The eucharist is certainly a time of worship. But in another sense, it moves you beyond time to a timeless expression of your relationship with God and of the blending of your life with the lives of other parishioners. Together you give thanks. And together you are called to be present—not in some attendance taking sort of way—but in all your senses: smell, touch, sight, hearing, taste, and in the depths of your heart. Then, as the liturgy unfolds, you may end up believing in God and others as the center of your life as you renew your faith in the one for whom Christians hunger.

People's Hungers

Explore what hunger means to you. Perhaps you have experienced one or more kinds of hunger in your life. Go deeper now. Imagine hunger(s) in your life. Pursue how you relieve them. Try to discover what you might do to relieve others' hungers as well.

- For me, hunger is . . .

____

____

____

____

- Other kinds of hunger might be . . .

____

____

____

____

As a way of exploring hunger further, read the excerpts that follow.

Going Hungry

Every day a half billion people go hungry; three times that number are chronically ill. Half the world's population does not have safe water. A third are unemployed or underemployed and at least that many lack shelter. Almost twenty million, mainly women and children, are refugees, and twenty-four million more are displaced within their own countries. A quarter of a million children die every week from hunger, disease, violence or neglect.[7]

Most Human of All Qualities

Some 2,000 years after Jesus fed the hungry, starvation continues to claim lives because people who can influence private and public policy don't seem to care enough about their malnourished brothers and sisters. They allow other considerations, such as national and international politics, land tenure and business profitability, to get in the way of addressing this most fundamental of human needs.

If this is true (and the logic seems inescapable), then the most deadly disease known to humankind (worse than cancer, heart disease and AIDS combined) is hardness of heart. People continue to die every day from war and famine because their fellow human beings have lost that most human of all qualities: compassion.[8]

- In your opinion, why is there so much hunger in the world?

____

____

____

____

The need for food is people's most basic physical need. How can one speak to a person about anything else when one's stomach aches and one's mouth is dry? Some people who are convinced of eternal life sometimes fail to see their responsibilities in this life. They may appear to forget or deny that Jesus walked on this earth, shared meals with others on numerous occasions, and filled many people's needs. Indeed, Jesus told his disciples: "I myself am the living bread that came down from heaven; whoever eats this bread will live forever; and the bread that I will give is my flesh for the life of the world" (John 6:51).

Perhaps what needs to be emphasized is the connection between physical and spiritual hungers. For a Christian, the link between them is the experience of the liturgy of the mass. Perhaps you may see this experience as being called not only to worship God with others, but also to go forth from this mystery to live justly in your everyday life. By thinking this way, you may be better able to identify with those who are without food. You may be able to begin to feel their basic needs, and they may begin to be able to feel yours. This means, of course, that you may end up revealing hungers in your own life. These hungers may have nothing to do with calories and carbohydrates, but with other basics, like peace, love, and happiness. Indeed, persons who are physically starving or malnourished may be able to help you discover what you really value in life.

- What hunger was there in your life that led you to inquire about becoming Christian? How has your experience of the rite of Christian initiation begun to fill this hunger?

____

____

____

____

Hunger and the Center of Life

Another way to understand hunger is to view it as the deepest longing of a person. You might say that this greatest hunger lies at the very center of who you are. As you look back on your life, you may uncover what it is that makes you who you are. This does not mean only trying to recall as much as you can of your past. That is part of life's journey, but not all of it. Rather, it means trying to discover your most intimate longings, your most hidden inner self. The past of your life is not behind you, but under you. It supports you and is part of your search, your journey of faith.

This search for what lies at the center of your life may not have begun with your entrance into the catechumenate. It may have started years before that. Or you may be beginning now, as a neophyte, to discover what you hunger for. This search may also be a painful one. Why do people take years to find their niche in a chosen career or job? Why do college students change majors? Why do people decide to join one organization over another? Or leave one for another?

The pain involved in seeking what you hunger for may sometimes appear to be more than you can bear. The help you gain from your relationships with others may be a strong support in coping with pain—and in enjoying life's pleasures. Perhaps you will eventually understand the pain you experience as characteristic of being an adult, and not something you can be rid of entirely for the rest of your life. In accepting the pain of life, along with its pleasures, you may be able to clarify what you really hunger for.

This search for the center, or that which lies at the root of who you are, is not something that only individuals go through. Governments, churches, educational institutions—these and other organizations may experience difficulty in finding what really makes them what they are.

One benefit of searching for what is at the center of your life is that of trying to uncover what you yearn for—what you hunger for—as a baptized person. By exploring who you are, you may be able to identify something about yourself you had not even thought of before. You may begin to understand better the hungers in your life, what you yearn for and will not live without.

Imagine beginning a journey to a place you sense you've visited but don't recall when or how. The only help you have is a companion who has already made a similar journey elsewhere. You don't know how you will get there, or what you will do once you arrive. As you start out, fearful yet eager, your companion says,

> No one on earth knows precisely what it means to "seek God" until he himself has set out to find Him. No one can tell another what this search means unless that other is enlightened, at the same time, by the Spirit speaking within his own heart. In the end, no one can seek God unless he has already begun to find Him. No one can find God without having first been found by Him.[9]

- These words, from Thomas Merton, deal with seeking God. What does it mean for you to seek God now?

____

____

____

____

A Journey to Eucharist: The Bread of Life

So far in this book you have explored a variety of the rites leading to baptism. Chapter 2 may have helped you to recall being plunged into the waters of rebirth. You may still sense the sparkling glow of the Easter candle, or tingle with the crispness of the shining garment that covered you.

There was more to come, however. More that you may have been hungering for, yearning for. Refreshed and reborn by water and the Spirit, you joined with your parish in the Church's sacrificial meal of new life, the eucharist. For newly baptized people, the eucharist is "the climax of their initiation and the center of the whole Christian life" (*RCIA*, #243).[10] The eucharist can be an ongoing source of nourishment for you and all who believe in Jesus as the Bread of Life. One newly baptized person recalled her first sharing in the eucharist this way:

> My biggest thing was to take part in the eucharist. ...I remember Father coming up to me [afterward] and saying there was like a light in me. He said I glowed the whole night...like he was sitting up on the altar and watching me...and that's how I felt....No matter what happened, nobody could take that feeling away from me.

- What do you recall of your first celebration of the eucharist? How did you feel?

____

____

____

____

Eucharist is a word that means thanksgiving. Christians pray in thanks for Jesus, the Bread of Life. Christians may say: "We pray in hope for this nourishment to sustain us in our daily lives. We pray that we may live as a Church community in which members provide mutual support and reach out beyond parish boundaries to deal with realities of everyday life." One key word here is the word "pray"; another is "we." In parishes where worshipers are scattered all over the church for mass, it may be difficult to sense or develop an awareness of group participation, or "we-ness." Still, the thanksgiving of eucharist is intended to be an expression of thanks from all assembled. The eucharist is not one person's nourishment for one hour a week; it is the parish's food for the whole week. In chapters 5, 6, and 7, the eucharistic celebration is presented to help you explore worship in your life as a newly baptized person and its link to how you live as a Christian.

- In light of what you have just read, what do you think hunger has to do with the eucharist?

  ___

  ___

  ___

  ___

- Recall the discussion of uncovering what is at the center of your life (page 102). Then discuss with one or two other people the last line in the scripture reading on page 90: "Your faith and hope, then, are centered in God."

Did You Know?

The call to peace, love, and service is an important dimension of the eucharist, and is grounded in the Old Testament. The source of this call, or hunger, is firmly rooted in Judaism. Centuries before Jesus, for example, the prophets urged people to be faithful to God. In the Old Testament we read:

> "Peace, peace!" they say,
> though there is no peace (Jeremiah 6:14b).
>
> Render true judgment, and show kindness and
> compassion toward each other (Zechariah 7:9).
>
> You have been told, O man, what is good,
> and what the Lord requires of you:
> Only to do the right and to love goodness,
> and to walk humbly with your God (Micah 6:8).

The way you act is not some added-on feature of being a Christian. The gift of Jesus in the eucharist calls you to act justly and be a person of peace. In the early Church, Christians were to show by the way they lived what they believed. According to Hippolytus of Rome, each neophyte was to:

> Be zealous to perform good works and to please God, living righteously, devoting himself to the Church, performing the things which he has learnt, advancing in the service of God.[11]

Later, in the fourth century, Ambrose of Milan would tell the newly baptized:

Can a man be a king of justice, when he himself is scarcely just; can he be a king of peace, when he can scarcely be peaceable?[12]

You have been born of water and the Spirit. You are united now to God and to other baptized persons. You share the mission to bear witness to what you believe—and whom you believe in—Jesus of Nazareth. Begin to participate more actively in this mission by doing the following, either for personal reflection or with a friend.

- Look up one of the following scripture passages. Write or discuss how the passage you choose might have relevance to your life.

Isaiah 2:1–5	Luke 4:16–30	Amos 5:14–15
Matthew 25:31–46	Isaiah 58:6	James 2:14–26

____

____

____

____

ACCEPTING THE CHALLENGE

Accepting the eucharist as central to your life may not be a simple yes/no decision for you. It may be a response shaped over a period of time with your parish. And you may never finish reviewing and redoing it.

"Who knows what pertains to a person except the spirit of the person that is within" (1 Corinthians 2:11)? Who knows, for sure, what lies at the depths of who you are? Who knows . . . really . . . who knows what moved you to embark on your catechumenal journey?

This chapter suggests that the greatest hunger may lie at the very center of who you are. Getting in touch with who you are is, of course, part of being a catechumen and now, a neophyte. It is also intended to lead you beyond your own needs, to look at needs that may exist around you. Now you are being asked to accept what the eucharist can become for your life. One dimension of this has to do with taking a stand. That can be difficult, especially for people who tend to be shy or uncertain about such things.

John Westerhoff points out that "there is no way to act like a Christian apart from being one, that is, apart from participation in the life of a Christian faith community, the church."[13] Membership in the church is not simply a matter of saying to oneself, "Well, if I have time I'll do this or that. After all, St. Lucy's has a full-time staff."

One of the most important aspects of being a catechumen may have been the feeling of support and care you felt from others: compassion and concern, healing and tenderness, openness and laughter. The support of the parish leading to baptism is also intended to lead you from baptism. Of course, this is the ideal. You may have had second thoughts about another parishioner, or wondered why a certain person had the role he or she had. The strength or weakness of how you relate to others will not change overnight. Hopefully, however, there is a foundation of support in your parish that can help you to become better informed about what makes your parish tick and what are its vital concerns. In other words, to help you see what is at the center of parish life.

Your becoming a Christian was really a process of becoming part of the fiber of a community of people who share a story of faith of which your own story is a part. You are invited to continue that story by gathering with others to come to the altar for the nourishment of the eucharist.

- One question for you to think about now is: How can this presence of Jesus to me in the eucharist help me to be a person of compassion, justice, and mercy? For example, if a catechumen you know needs a sponsor, will you volunteer? Why or why not?

- What other work will you do? Parishioners in many parishes provide transportation to local residents on a regular basis. Give one specific thing you might do to help others where you live.

Looking Back

> A week later I realized what happened. At that time it was like a blank...like your wedding day, you don't remember it all, you know? Because it takes time to sink in, it really does...to me anyway...and when it did sink in, it was a tremendous experience...the love I felt...everyone that spent the time with me to help me, to lead me, to encourage me, and everything...it was great ...when it sank in!

The above is how one newly baptized person described his experience of the Easter Vigil. Focus now on your experience of the vigil, particularly your sharing in the eucharist on the night of your baptism.

Review briefly the sections on the scriptures (pages 86-98) and on renewing your life of faith (pages 98-106). Remember your sharing in the sacraments of initiation that culminated in your first sharing of the eucharist. Whatever you choose to do, make this central part of the faith into which you were baptized more thoroughly your own.

For the scriptures for the third Sunday of the Easter season, consider the following.

- Acts of the Apostles 2:14, 22–28—People may stand up for what they believe in a variety of ways. One person may "speak with his or her feet," and decide to leave an organization. Another may quietly but relentlessly work for some personal goal. Still another may welcome confrontation with people with whom he or she disagrees. Now answer for yourself: One way I can stand up for what I believe in is by...

  ____

  ____

  ____

  ____

- 1 Peter 1:17–21—Some people feel that prayer and action are separate ways of living their faith. Others suggest that they are part of a single fabric of faith. My opinion is . . .

- Luke 23:13–35—How welcome might a stranger feel in my parish? Why? Will I try to ensure that there is a spirit of hospitality?

For the section on renewing your life of faith (pages 98-106), ask yourself:

- How can I relate my sharing in eucharist with my parish to the practical realities and problems I face every day?

Read the following comments, and answer the questions that follow.

> I don't buy it. All they do is go there [to church] for an hour, race out of the parking lot, and forget what it means to act like a Christian the rest of the week. I'd rather not be a hypocrite, so I don't go anymore.

- If someone says the above to me, what will I say?

____

____

____

____

> My children are hungry. There's been another cutback in the aid program, and I barely have enough for my family to survive. Sometimes I feel so discouraged. I feel so down and out. I thought even a visit to church would help, but it was all locked up. I don't know where to turn.

- What would I say to this person?

____

____

____

____

As you conclude this chapter on the center of your life of faith, you may want to pray these words of David in Psalm 16:

> Keep me safe, O God;
> in you I take refuge.
> I say to the LORD,
> you are my LORD. . . .
> LORD, my allotted portion and my cup,
> you have made my destiny secure. . . .
>
> You will show me the path to life,
> abounding joy in your presence,
> the delights at your right hand forever.

If you wish, complete your prayer with the following:

Lord, you show us the path of life.

Be present to me, so that I may ______________________________

____

____

Lord, you show us the path of life.

Be present to my parish, so that we may ________________________

____

____

4

The Fullness of Your Life of Faith

Psalm–Prayer

The Lord is my shepherd;
    there is nothing I lack.
In green pastures you let me graze;
    to safe waters you lead me;
    you restore my strength.
You guide me along the right path
    for the sake of your name.
Even when I walk through a dark valley,
    I fear no harm for you are at my side;
    your rod and staff give me courage.

You set a table before me
    as my enemies watch;
You anoint my head with oil;
    my cup overflows.
Only goodness and love will pursue me
    all the days of my life;
I will dwell in the house of the Lord
    for years to come.

Psalm 23:1–6

Overview

Fullness of life is the theme for chapter 4. Throughout the chapter you may find yourself engaged in a mental tug-of-war about what fullness of life means to you. Perhaps you would describe the liturgy of your baptism as an experience of the fullness of life—a high point after months or years of preparation. Or fullness of life may be an ongoing sense of coming to know more about yourself, Jesus, and how you relate to others. It may be no more than saying "Aha!" to some new insight or some hidden and indescribable meaning associated with an experience you've had. However you may describe fullness of life now, this chapter may help you discover what it can be for you in light of your baptism.

Discussing parts of this chapter or its various activities with others might yield some new avenues for you to explore, as well as enable you to clarify more effectively what fullness of life means for your life now. It may be quite beneficial to talk with someone who was baptized years ago. Use the space provided throughout the chapter if you wish to respond to the suggested activities.

EXPLORING YOUR EXPERIENCE

Fullness of life can be, for a Christian, an important awareness of the experience of Christ in one's life. It may be an overarching sense of what the meaning and purpose of one's life are.

The photographs that follow may help you to begin to discover what fullness of life means for you. Look at the photographs, and the accompanying words of Jesus, and then answer the questions that follow.

"I came

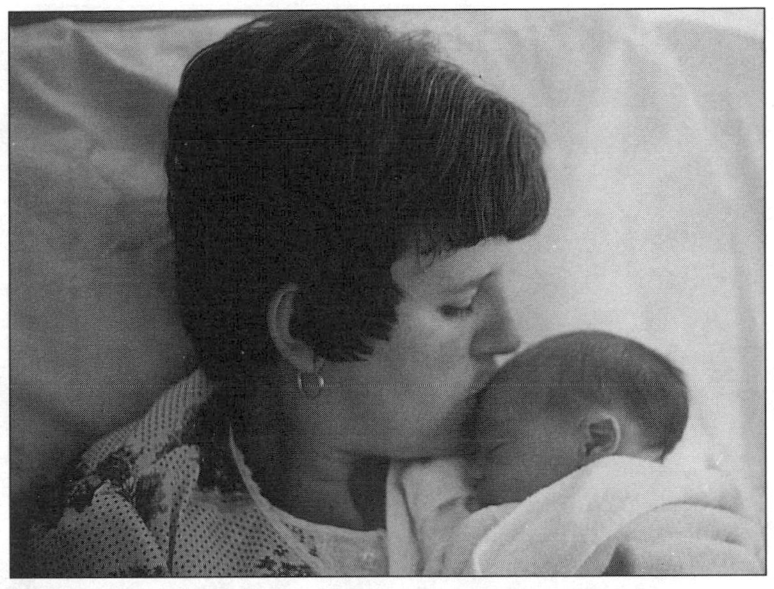

that they might have life

and have it to the full."

- What memories do these photographs trigger from your life? How do you feel about these memories now?

____

____

____

____

Fullness of life: what is it?

For a child it may be the first time riding on a bicycle, or being welcomed into the neighborhood group as a "regular."

The Personals column of the classified section of a newspaper gives a glimpse of how adults might view fullness of life:

> Sam. Thank you for coming back to me. I need you and love you. Love, Marianne.
>
> Amy, I have alway loved you and always will. You are life to me. I will return to you someday, and will never leave you or the kids again. Please contact me.

For others it may be the dream of a new start in a new land, a new beginning following bankruptcy proceedings, or a feeling of exhilaration after a medical lab test comes back negative.

For some Christians, fullness of life may be directly related to a blossoming prayer life. One may participate in a prayer group or parish devotions, or develop a personal prayer style that is particularly fulfilling.

Even with suggestions from other people's experiences, it may be difficult to determine what fullness of life may mean for you today. Advertisers promote all kinds of products that promise fulfillment or success. People struggle mercilessly to reach personal goals, and, when they finally do, are sometimes disappointed. One can almost hear them asking: "Is that all there is?"

For a Christian, like you, fullness of life can mean a deeper awareness of how you relate to Christ. It may be a better grasp of your role in the parish. It may be taking a stand on the construction of a local nuclear power plant. It may be similar to other people's experiences, perhaps even like some of those mentioned above.

- If you were asked to explain about the fullness of life to a person inquiring about becoming Christian, what would you say? Try to be as practical as possible.

____

____

____

____

The following remarks of a newly baptized person may provide another way of looking at fullness of life:

> The other night we were talking about [trying to find Jesus] and someone said finding him in a neighbor that she has a hard time—has difficulty—getting along with. And I found myself thinking of different instances or different people where I could see Christ in that person, or that person trying to put him on in a positive way. Before I had any of this experience [of the catechumenate] or this knowledge or learning on my part, it was always a black or white type of thing: "This is the way it was, or this is the way it is." Now I can see into things more.

Perhaps seeing into things more is one part of what yearning for the fullness of life is all about. Your baptism and first sharing in the eucharist may become, then, a continuation of a journey already begun. Conversion continues, then, as a process of seeing into things more.

Read again the comment of the newly baptized person above. Then look at the situations in the first column of the chart that follows. The corresponding statement in the second column is one obvious comment a person in each situation might make. In the third column, enter what you think the person might *really* be saying about one or more of the situations.

Searching for Hidden Meanings

Situation	*Comment*	*Possible Hidden Meaning*
Breakup with a friend	"It doesn't matter; she was moving."	
A wedding anniversary	"We made it; 15 years today."	
Lack of participation by people at mass	"They should be happy I come."	
Saying no to a child	"My kid always wants stuff from me."	
Bishops' involvement in peace and justice issues	"They should leave politics to the politicians."	
Conflict at work	"Why do they pick on me all the time?"	
Uncertainty over a moral issue	"It's all black and white to me."	

Trying to see into things more may help a baptized person, like you, believe in Jesus. Indeed, insights provided by biblical accounts and Church teachings about him support your growth in faith. Think back to the night of your baptism. The celebrant asked if you believed in:

- God, the Father almighty
- Jesus Christ, his only Son
- the Holy Spirit
- the holy catholic Church
- the communion of saints
- the forgiveness of sins
- the resurrection of the body
- life everlasting

Knowing the basic truths of Christian belief is, of course, important. But remember that you were asked if you believed in them. Developing an attitude of faith, now that you are baptized, means trying to see into things more. This may enable you to see for yourself who Jesus is for your life.

EXPLORING THE SCRIPTURES

The focus in this chapter is on fullness of life, especially in relation to your experience of baptism. Your journey of faith has taken you to baptism and beyond. Your initiation into the Christian faith may be continuing now as you pray and meet with others in your parish. Perhaps you are thinking about becoming more active in parish life, or about continuing some service you performed while you were a catechumen.

In the experience of everyday life, you may begin to discover more about Jesus. For Christians, Jesus is the way to life with God that is beyond any ending in time. It is a fullness of life for all time. Try to recall what has led you to faith in Jesus and membership in the Church. Recall the liturgy of your baptism, and what prompted you to become Christian.

- What do you remember from the past week that tells you of your need for God?

____

____

____

____

The Scriptures of the Fourth Sunday of Easter

The first two readings for the fourth Sunday of Easter are from the same books of the New Testament that you have seen in several previous chapters: the Acts of the Apostles and the first letter of Peter. The gospel reading is from the gospel according to John. It is the first Sunday gospel passage of this season that does not describe an appearance of Jesus following the resurrection.

ACTS OF THE APOSTLES 2:14, 36–41

This reading includes another part of Peter's address on Pentecost. An earlier part (2:14, 22–28) appeared in the third chapter of this book. Peter asserts that his audience must reform and be baptized in the name of Jesus Christ. Imagine how much has been written and said over twenty centuries in the name of Jesus Christ! Some might say that no other name is used so frequently for such a wide variety of purposes: for example, in prayer, in anger, in teaching. In its most basic meaning, Jesus means "God saves" and Christ, "the anointed one." As you read the passage, think of what you mean when you say the name Jesus Christ. Try to recall how you felt when you heard Jesus' name during the liturgy of your baptism.

[On the day of Pentecost] Peter stood up with the Eleven, raised his voice, and addressed them: "Let the whole house of Israel know beyond any doubt that God has made both Lord and Messiah this Jesus whom you crucified."

When they heard this, they were deeply shaken. They asked Peter and the other apostles, "What are we to do, brothers?" Peter answered: "You must reform and be baptized, each one of you, in the name of Jesus Christ, that your sins may be forgiven; then you will receive the gift of the Holy Spirit. It was to you and your children that the promise was made, and to all those still far off whom the Lord our God calls."

In support of his testimony he used many other arguments, and kept urging, "Save yourselves from this generation which has gone astray." Those who accepted his message were baptized; some three thousand were added that day.

This passage presents the pattern of Christian initiation in the New Testament: evangelization of the inquirers, leading to conversion and baptism. Perhaps your experience of becoming a Christian followed a similar process.

Peter's call to reform one's life and to be baptized is linked to the forgiveness of sins. This repentance is to be taken as a change of heart, a turning to Jesus, whom "God has made both Lord and Messiah." The gift of the Spirit is also closely associated with the individual's baptism. The Spirit given in baptism is indeed the Spirit promised by the risen Christ (Acts 2:33). Luke, author of the Acts of the Apostles, says in the gospel also attributed to him that Jesus returned from his baptism in the Jordan River "filled with the holy Spirit" (4:1). The Spirit was a source of strength and power for Jesus.

Perhaps you may want to recall now the strength and power of the Spirit in your life. Begin to do this by remembering the liturgy of your baptism. The liturgy began with the celebrant saying something like the following to the assembly:

> Dear friends, let us pray to almighty God for our brothers and sisters, N. and N., who are asking for baptism. He has called them and brought them to this moment; may he grant them light and strength to follow Christ with resolute hearts and to profess the faith of the Church. May he give them the new life of the Holy Spirit, whom we are about to call down on this water (*RCIA*, #220).[1]

The turning to Jesus of the newly baptized may be understood as a gradual awareness of the Spirit, prompting one to seek, investigate, learn, and discover the fullness of life.

Complete the sentences below and discuss your responses with others if you wish.

- For me, the Spirit is like ______________________________

____

- For me, the gift of the Spirit in baptism means ____________________

  ____

- When I was baptized, I felt ____________________

  ____

1 PETER 2:20–25

This reading is directed to workers who often served under severe masters. Peter does not address the social evil of slavery, but discusses the manner in which the follower of Christ is called to accept sufferings at the hands of unjust people. The model for such a worker is Jesus, the suffering servant.

If you put up with suffering for doing what is right, this is acceptable in God's eyes. It was for this you were called, since Christ suffered for you in just this way and left you an example, to have you follow in his footsteps. He did no wrong; no deceit was found in his mouth. When he was insulted he returned no insult. When he was made to suffer, he did not counter with threats. Instead, he delivered himself up to the One who judges justly. In his own body he brought your sins to the cross, so that all of us, dead to sin, could live in accord with God's will. By his wounds you were healed. At one time you were straying like sheep, but now you have returned to the shepherd, the guardian of your souls.

Frequently, situations of suffering are "settled" by violent means. Police may storm an apartment house when a family member threatens others because he or she can't take the pressure of family life anymore. Oppressed people around the world struggle for peaceful solutions, but often, violence erupts. The suffering of a strained relationship between a couple may result in abuse or verbal threats.

Peter rejects all violence, even when it might be justified in the opinion of the oppressed. He urges his readers to remember that Christ suffered for them, doing so willingly on the cross. Through Christ's death, Christians are reconciled with God. By Christ's wounds, others are healed. His followers are called to follow Christ's example. Recall these words of John Chrysostom, who encouraged newly baptized people this way in the fourth century:

> Imitate him [Christ], I beg you, and you will be able to be called newly baptized not only for two, three, ten, or twenty days, but you will be able to deserve this greeting after ten, twenty, or thirty years have passed and, to tell the truth, through your whole life.[2]

The imitation of Christ and the acceptance of suffering can be as challenging today as they were centuries ago. How is a baptized person to imitate Christ and to deal with suffering in the world today? Certainly a Christian is to try to work with others to alleviate suffering. Think of suffering in your family, town, or anywhere else: accidents that take the lives of innocent people; a report of a bomb going off in the Mideast; a hurricane or flood slamming coastal towns, or an earthquake shattering buildings and dreams with a minute's rumblings; synagogues and churches being desecrated. To live in the fullness of life is to recognize life's pitfalls as well as triumphs, and to assist in correcting the former while rejoicing in the latter.

As a newly baptized person, you have already expressed belief in Jesus as Son of God, Lord and Savior, Second Person of the Trinity. Now you might want to explore further who Jesus is and what he means for your life. The challenge is to live in discipleship with others as members of the Church, doing the best you can with your own abilities, moved by the Spirit of the risen Lord. This means working to know more about who you are, what you are about. In essence, it means trying to discover ever so gently Jesus' continuing presence in your life. You may want to complete one or more of the following to help you do this.

- "I don't buy that Jesus stuff. I don't believe Jesus is the Son of God." If someone said this to me, I would say that Jesus . . .

  ____

  ____

  ____

  ____

- The next time you visit a mall or shopping center, observe the expressions on the faces of people as they go about their business. Do you see suffering in their faces? Hope? What else might you see? Why is that?

  ____

  ____

  ____

  ____

- The most difficult suffering to deal with may be one's own. Are you suffering now? If you are, what are you doing about it?

  ____

  ____

  ____

  ____

You might want to discuss this reading and what it can mean for you today with others. If you do, use one of the following exercises to get the discussion started.

- Read Isaiah 53 on the suffering servant. Then ask the group to discuss what this passage might have to do with the reading from 1 Peter 2:20–25. Conclude by discussing practical implications for your group.

- Read the following statement from the U.S. bishops' reflection ten years after their pastoral letter, *The Challenge of Peace*. Then discuss the questions that follow.

> "In our day, the Holy Spirit continues to call us to seek peace with one another, so that in our peacemaking we may prepare for the coming of the reign of God, a kingdom of true justice, love and peace."[3]

What could "our peacemaking" mean? What does peace have to do with imitating Jesus? Why?

What does peace have to do with suffering in your parish? Why?

- Discuss attitudes people may have toward suffering:

> Why does God allow it?
> Suffering can make you strong.
> People bring it on themselves.

Conclude by asking the group to decide if there is value in suffering "with" another person. Discuss how one might do this.

JOHN 10:1–10

This passage comes just before the well-known words of Jesus, "I am the good shepherd" (verse 11). In the gospel passage you are about to read, Jesus is both shepherd and gate to the sheepfold. These were common images to the people of Jesus' time, and it was not so unusual for Jesus to talk about them. Although these things are not so immediately present to us, the power of the story is just as valid for Christians today. As you read the passage, try to recall what motivated you to place your faith in Jesus before you were baptized.

Jesus said:

"Truly I assure you:
Whoever does not enter the sheepfold through the gate
but climbs in some other way
is a thief and a marauder.
The one who enters through the gate
is shepherd of the sheep;
the keeper opens the gate for him.
The sheep hear his voice
as he calls his own by name
and leads them out.
When he has brought out [all] those that are his,
he walks in front of them,
and the sheep follow him
because they recognize his voice.
They will not follow a stranger;
such a one they will flee,
because they do not recognize a stranger's voice."

Even though Jesus used this figure with them, they did not grasp what he was trying to tell them. He therefore said [to them again]:

"My solemn word is this:
I am the sheepgate.
All who came before me
were thieves and marauders
whom the sheep did not heed.

"I am the gate.
Whoever enters through me
will be safe.
He will go in and out,
and find pasture.
The thief comes
only to steal and slaughter and destroy.
I came
that they might have life
and have it to the full."

Jesus' words are addressed to religious leaders who were not seeing eye to eye with him. In this passage the leaders are compared to thieves who refuse to enter the fold through the gate. Jesus' words, however, can be addressed to all people and not just to the audience John the evangelist chose to write about.

Jesus is not just a shepherd here, but the gate to the sheepfold as well. He not only leads his followers to fullness of life, but that life can be found in him. The one who responds to Jesus the shepherd will "find pasture": sharing in the life of God.

One informative aspect of this parable is the sense of intimacy and care that the shepherd has for his sheep. The response of the sheep to the shepherd is not automatic; they must first hear his voice.

Today, one may feel pressure to listen to many different voices. For example, newspaper headlines may tell us:

Furor Surrounds Teen Center
Elderly Couple Begs Doctor: Let Us Die
AIDS Children: School Controversy Widens

These examples merely suggest some voices people may hear as they try to live as people of faith. Other voices may be closer to home. For example, you may be torn between the opinions of a friend and a spouse on how to resolve a long-standing conflict with a neighbor. You may be struggling to get close to a lonely relative, to really understand, to listen as attentively as you can. But you sense nothing happens. You may feel that you're at a dead end. What do you do?

It may be tempting to think, "If only I were more like Jesus, I'd be able to. . . ." For a baptized person, the challenge is to accept Jesus of Nazareth as the one who calls you to hope in the future—indeed, a timeless future—as you face the practical circumstances of everyday life. It may be easy sometimes to forget that Jesus did not always have a receptive audience. He was rejected, not once but twice in his hometown of Nazareth (John 4:43–54; Mark 6:1–6); was persecuted for curing a man on the sabbath (John 5:1–18); and was scolded for forgiving the sins of the paralytic (Luke 5:17–26). Your willingness to be baptized may have been for you a sign of your trust in God's mercy and a decision to face with hope the hard issues of life, on several levels—personal or social, parish or town, nation or world. This willingness alone can be a response in faith to the one who promised fullness of life. As God was with the prophets, so is God with you: "I have called you by name: you are mine" (Isaiah 43:1).

In chapter 1, it was suggested that faith involves one's whole attitude toward God and one's notion of what it means to communicate with others in the world. In light of this, ask yourself:

- Are there people with whom I am unable to communicate? Why is that? What might I do about it?

____

____

____

____

- Using your own examples, indicate how you may shy away from things you know are really important.

____

____

____

____

- Imagine yourself at a parish council meeting shortly after your baptism. The parish council president thanks you for coming and expresses hope that you will participate as the meeting goes on. How do you feel about speaking up?

___

___

___

___

RENEWING YOUR LIFE OF FAITH

One of the principal beliefs of Christianity is the belief in the presence of the risen Christ in the Church. Jesus calls his followers to share in the life he came to bring in all its fullness. The Church frequently has looked to the letters of Paul for uncovering what it means to be "Church." Paul writes, for example, "So we, though many, are one body in Christ and individually parts of one another" (Romans 12:5). Later, when Paul's thoughts on the union of Christians with Christ are more developed, he will write: "He [Christ] is the head of the body, the church" (Colossians 1:18).

To be a member of a community that stands for some things and against others is part of what it means to belong to the Church. To be part of the Church excludes certain values and attitudes. Indeed, the Church's bishops are called to be shepherds to those whom they serve.

One newly baptized person speaks of his beginning experience with the Church and coming to baptism as gradually discovering "a new direction in life." Could this also be a gradual experience of fullness of life? As you met with others in your parish and prepared for baptism, you may have thought about your purpose in life in a new way. You may have become more aware of some difficulties in how you relate to a friend, or of a new insight into a conflict that had gone unsettled. There may have been a sense of sin in your life, and a need for healing that previously had gone unnoticed. Whatever your personal situation was, you continued to prepare for baptism. In the spirit of looking back on your baptism, read these words of Ambrose of Milan to the newly baptized:

> You went, you washed, you came to the altar, you began to see what you had not seen before. That is: Through the font of the Lord and the preaching of the Lord's passion, your eyes were then opened. You who seemed before to have been blind in heart began to see the light of the sacraments.[4]

One may wonder if Ambrose had in mind the exchange between Jesus and the man born blind (John 9:1–41) when he delivered this sermon. Ambrose's mentioning being "blind in heart" is more than a physical blindness, but an inner blindness. Recall this part of the story of the man born blind. Jesus asked the man he had healed:

> "Do you believe in the Son of Man?" He answered and said, "Who is he, sir, that I may believe in him?" Jesus said to him, "You have seen him and the one speaking with you is he." He said, "I do believe, Lord," and he worshiped him (John 9: 35–38).

Jesus helps people to see beyond the obvious. They are able, gradually, to see into things more and believe in him. Perhaps Jesus is really after people to develop an attitude of faith in him. As the sightless see, so too others who can see will be blind to this light, refusing to see beyond the obvious.

Ambrose's words may help you to discover what the fullness of life of baptism can mean for you. His speaking of beginning to see what was not seen before seems to parallel the description of baptism as a "new direction in life" and seeing beyond the obvious already mentioned here.

Read the following poem about a person preparing for baptism. It tells of an older person who decided to inquire about becoming Christian, who may have been seeking a new direction in life.

He Was

He was to be baptized at an age that
most people would say was too, too
old, but he was determined that it
would take place, so it was set into
motion, first the father of the beloved
name, then the sister of the starry
night, who spoke in a tongue that
knew not the dark of it, but its
beauty, all was now set, five
were standing by to do their
thing, in this case, the water flowing
on a brow. The incantations were said,
in a sing-song voice that rose to
new heights, all were joyous, rightly
so, the foot prints of time were etched
in a size that was not mistaken, he was a
man born again, the father smiled, approvingly.[5]

Determination. Joy. Anticipation. Eagerness. These are just a few words that might describe the feelings of the person of faith whom this poem is about. Can you think of other possible feelings? What are they?

____

____

____

____

He was too old, some would say, to be baptized. But why? After all, it was such a simple act: in the pouring of the water it was done. Not some magical rite, but a sign of life in all its fullness, a curious blend of reality and mystery, merging and making the man who was "too, too old" a child of God (see 1 John 3:1).

Entry into the Church

During the celebration of your baptism, one important theme you may have heard about was your entry into the faith of the Church. Moved by the Spirit of God, the Church is to be a sign of God's love in the world. The Church, which probably became a part of your life long before baptism, is a people who share "one Lord, one faith, one baptism" (Ephesians 4:5).

The responsibility of the Church, and in particular of your parish, all during the catechumenate was to demonstrate its hospitality and nourish your ongoing conversion in faith. How wrong it would have been to baptize you and then let go of you! Your entry into the faith of the Church was an entry into a Church called to support all who were preparing for baptism.

The Church calls on not just its present members, but on all who have gone before. You may recall that soon after the beginning of the liturgy of your baptism, a litany of saints was sung. This litany, which came just before the blessing of the baptismal water, invoked the aid of the saints for you who were seeking baptism.

In the chart labeled with names of saints below, enter the names of whomever you now wish to remember as you look back on your baptism. Perhaps these people have been saint-like to you, and you may want to thank them in prayer and in person for their support of what may have been a new direction in life for you.

Saints Past and Present

Mary	Teresa of Avila	Peter
John		Mark
Mary Magdalene		Clare
Francis of Assisi		Catherine
Luke	Elizabeth Ann Seton	Paul

Entering into the faith of the Church also involves sharing in a vision and hope of what your parish can be, and deciding to become a part of it. One newly baptized person, in looking back on her experience as a catechumen, has remarked:

> Even before baptism I already felt that I was an accepted part of it [the parish community]. . . . I was excited about the whole thing. . . . As time went on, it really reassured me that this was something I really wanted.

A newly baptized person, like you, ordinarily experiences a gradual entry into the life of the Church. With the passage of time, you may have felt more a part of the parish you were joining. You may have had moments of joy but also times of disappointment. Still, you maintained your spiritual preparation, journeying toward the font—your doorway to the eucharistic table.

Water and Fullness of Life

The joy and excitement of your baptism may have resulted in a lasting memory for you. The whole parish may have applauded spontaneously as you were immersed or the water was poured over you for the third time. What power of water is this, that one's life can be so dramatically changed? How is this water, poured in the liturgy of baptism, a vehicle for sharing in the fullness of life?

To help you answer these questions, recall the prayer of blessing of the water when you were baptized. The celebrant blessed the water, singing in part:

> Father,
> look now with love upon your Church
> and unseal for it the fountain of baptism.
>
> By the power of the Holy Spirit
> give to this water the grace of your Son,
> so that in the sacrament of baptism
> all those whom you have created in your likeness
> may be cleansed from sin
> and rise to a new birth of innocence
> by water and the Holy Spirit (*RCIA*, #222).[6]

The power of the water is rooted in the newness of life of the Spirit of the risen Christ. As you think about your baptism, perhaps your memory will be of people in your parish who helped you to prepare for your sharing in the life of Christ. Perhaps reflecting this way will provide you with a glimpse of what fullness of life can be for a Christian. It may help you to uncover something you have yet to consider regarding your "new birth of innocence."

One's new birth is not in seclusion, but in the presence of others who beckoned you to join them. John Chrysostom tells of the joy of the whole Church in his remarks on the incorporation of the newly baptized into the life of Christ:

I see that your gathering is brighter than usual today and the Church is rejoicing over her children....

Let us, then, rejoice with her and share her gladness.[7]

With help from catechists, sponsors, parishioners, and priests, you may have been overwhelmed by all the attention you may have received during the catechumenate. Being able to get to know such people and pray with them may have been something you began to count on before your baptism. The prayer and help of all these people are symbols of the life of the Church. It is one way of showing that the Church is alive in your parish, eager to aid persons inquiring about joining and to care for those who are already members.

Perhaps you assisted in one or more parish projects before your baptism. Now that you are baptized, your role is no less important. "With the help of their godparents," the newly baptized are now called to "experience a full and joyful welcome into the community and enter into closer ties with the other faithful" (*RCIA*, #246).[8] The faithful, those already baptized, can, with your help, remain full of faith. Who knows, support of just one of these parishioners by a newly baptized person, like you, may become a turning point in another's life. As one newly baptized person put it, "I look at my baptism as a commitment to God. To love God. To be good to people, to better myself."

Try to recall your first feelings about joining the Church.

- What did you see that attracted you to this community?

____

____

____

____

- What did you see that may have delayed you?

- What puzzled you?

- How do you feel now about your parish? Is there something you would like to change? Something you like just the way it is? What will you do about it?

Did You Know?

One of the basic aspects of baptism is that of communication: the communication between God and the parish; people with one another; people and God. The sacraments of the Church are, in a certain way, symbols that communicate. Through them, the Christian experiences the power and wonder of God. For example, water symbolizes the rebirth of the baptized. This basic level of communication with God can become a foundation for how you relate to and communicate with others. Reflect now on how you communicate with family, friends, or on the job. Complete one or more of the following to get you started.

- I show I (am) (am not) open to new ideas by . . .

  ____

  ____

  ____

  ____

- One person who is an example for me of the power and wonder of God is ____________________. For some reason, this person just enables me to . . .

  ____

  ____

  ____

  ____

- To help a person I know who may be experiencing a difficult personal situation I might . . .

  ____

  ____

  ____

  ____

Reflecting on how you communicate can help you to become confident in the faith you profess. It can help you to live by the light of the sacraments.

ACCEPTING THE CHALLENGE

Do you remember hearing the words that follow during the Easter Vigil? The Easter candle had been lighted, and the congregation may have also set the church aglow with burning candles. Several readers may have traced the story of God's love for his people through the ages. Then came the reading from Paul's letter to the Romans (6:3–11). Read it now, slowly, thoughtfully.

Are you not aware that we who were baptized into Christ Jesus were baptized into his death? Through baptism into his death we were buried with him, so that, just as Christ was raised from the dead by the glory of the Father, we too might live a new life. If we have been united with him through likeness to his death, so shall we be through a like resurrection. This we know; our old self was crucified with him so that the sinful body might be destroyed and we might be slaves to sin no longer. A man who is dead has been freed from sin. If we have died with Christ, we believe that we are also to live with him. We know that Christ, once raised from the dead, will never die again; death has no more power over him. His death was death to sin, once for all; his life is life for God. In the same way, you must consider yourselves dead to sin but alive for God in Christ Jesus.

This reading is a reflection on the meaning of baptism. The fathers of the Church of the fourth century saw in this passage an important resource for explaining to the newly baptized what had occurred in the immersion into the water of baptism. They saw in Paul's letter to the Romans an excellent resource for helping the newly baptized understand what they had experienced.

Cyril of Jerusalem delivered his sermons to the newly baptized in the Church of the Resurrection, built over what was believed to be the tomb of Jesus. Imagine the feelings of the newly baptized as they heard Cyril say:

You were conducted to the second pool of divine Baptism, as Christ passed from the cross to the sepulchre you see before you. You were asked, one by one, whether you believed in the name of the Father and of the Son and of the Holy Spirit; you made that saving confession, and then you dipped thrice under the water and thrice rose up again, therein mystically signifying Christ's three days' burial. For as our Savior passed three days and three nights in the bowels of the earth, so you by your first rising out of the water represented Christ's first day in the earth, and by your descent the night.... Your death coincided with your birth.

The strange, the extraordinary, thing is that we did not really die, nor were really buried or really crucified; nor did we really rise again: this was figurative and symbolic; yet our salvation was real. Christ's crucifixion was real, His burial was real, and His resurrection was real; and all these He has freely made ours, that by sharing His sufferings in a symbolic enactment we may really and truly gain salvation. Oh, too generous love![9]

These words of Cyril, as well as the passage from Paul to the Romans, are full of symbolism. Think for a moment about symbols around us today, such as those listed in the table that follows.

Some of Today's Symbols

Symbol	*Possible Meaning*
plaque on wall	personal or group achievement
flag	freedom, patriotism, territory
heart	"I love..."
handshake, embrace	warmth, caring, peace

Symbols often point to something more than their obvious meaning. What do the following symbols, all of which relate to your baptism, mean to you now?

- Water ______________________________

  ____

  ____

- Darkness ______________________________

  ____

  ____

- Light ______________________________

  ____

  ____

Looking Back

As you look back on your journey of initiation into the Church, try to recall memories that go beyond the words that were spoken. Focus, too, on what led you to receive the Spirit of God in your life. Recall your emotions, your joys, your tears. In other words, look at the whole you, rather than only what lies within your mind. Search out the Spirit deep within your heart.

The joy of the baptized is not a naive good feeling by which a Christian is able to avoid the hard issues of life: issues like accepting oneself; wounded relationships; children who desert their parents; or parents who desert their children. A Christian may also be puzzled over why a friend seems to undergo one terrible loss after another; or why a baby is born with a congenital birth defect; or being unable to leave words behind and hold a loved one. The joy of the baptized is a convincing yes to life in all its struggles and difficulties—in all its fullness. It is more of a joyful attitude conceived in the heart. Rather than an escape, it is an acceptance of life's problems in a spirit pregnant with hope and trust, confident that the Spirit of God is with you and your faith community.

Review now some of the main points of the section on the scriptures (pages 120-130). You may want to look again at one part that caught your eye. Or you may feel challenged by a particular phrase or explanation. You may even begin to look differently at what you believe in. As you begin, pray for a spirit of openness in your heart. May your attitude be one of deep joy and longing for the fullness of life.

For the scriptures of the fourth Sunday of Easter, ask yourself the following.

- Acts of the Apostles 2:14, 36–41—What or whom do I sometimes take for granted? What will I do about it?

  ____

  ____

  ____

  ____

- 1 Peter 2:20–25—How might I help others to reject violence as a solution to problems in society today?

  ____

  ____

  ____

  ____

- John 10:1–10—From what I have experienced so far, what would I say about the challenge of being a shepherd in the Church today?

  ____

  ____

  ____

  ____

For the section on entering into the faith of the Church (pages 130-139), think about various needs people have that lead them to join religious groups. Then complete the following.

- The greatest disappointment I have had to face as a baptized person is . . .

____

____

____

____

- One of the greatest joys I have had since my baptism is . . .

____

____

____

____

- Ask two or three people from your parish why they remain part of the Church. Encourage them to go beyond obvious reasons you would expect from a Christian. Then ask yourself what you think will cause you to remain a Christian. Discuss what you found with others if you wish.

Conclude this chapter as you began it. Look at the scripture passage and the photographs on pages 115-116: "I came that they might have life and have it to the full." In the space that follows, paste one or two photographs or draw a picture of what your sharing in the fullness of life in baptism is for you. If your choice involves another person (or persons), tell why you have made that choice. Rejoice in the gift of new life that is yours!

5

The Way, Truth, and Life of Faith

PSALM–PRAYER

Rejoice, you just, in the LORD;
    praise from the upright is fitting.
Give thanks to the LORD on the harp;
    on the ten-stringed lyre offer praise. . . .
For the LORD'S word is true;
    all his works are trustworthy.
The LORD loves justice and right
    and fills the earth with goodness. . . .

But the LORD'S eyes are upon the reverent,
    upon those who hope for his gracious help,
Delivering them from death,
    keeping them alive in times of famine.

Psalm 33: 1–2, 4–5, 18–19

Overview

Have you ever been in a situation where you found yourself saying something like this: "I am going to..." or "I am not about to..." or "I am hoping that..."? This fifth chapter provides you with the opportunity to explore one of Jesus' "I am..." statements: "I am the way, and the truth, and the life." The chapter may help you explore what Jesus' words can mean for your life and may even help you to see more possibilities for living as a Christian.

The chapter also invites you to continue to reflect on how you relate to Jesus in light of your celebration of the eucharist. The variety of activities may help you to think about, or rethink, your attitudes toward worship and its effect on your everyday life. Perhaps something you read or write here will be a source of encouragement for your journey of faith.

You may also come across sections you may want to review again, or about which you feel uncertain. Remember, the chapter is intended to help you clarify what you may believe and challenge you to consider what may be new ways of looking at the faith into which you were baptized.

Exploring Your Experience

As a newly baptized person, you are invited to discover how Jesus is your way, your truth, and your life.

Read the following imaginary dialogue between a TV talk show host and a caller who is seeking direction in life. Then continue with the paragraphs and questions that follow.

> *TV talk show host:* Is the caller there? (Silence) Is the caller there?
>
> *Caller:* Yes, I'm here. I'm just a little nervous.
>
> *Host:* Well, that's OK. Aren't we all sometimes? What's your question?
>
> *Caller:* I... I'm not sure how to ask this, but I'll try. Your guest today—the psychologist—says in her book that if you feel depressed a lot, you should try to get help. Well, a year ago I lost my husband, and I still feel so bad, even now. There's no meaning in life for me anymore. I don't know where to turn. I've thought about getting help, but I'm too embarrassed to call. My family tells me to snap out of it, but nothing works. I thought your guest, the doctor, could help.

Host: Doctor, what can you do for this caller? She's obviously upset. What do you suggest?

Doctor: In the limited time we have here, I would only say . . .

This imaginary situation deals with a person seeking advice on how to live. Determining how you are to live is part of your search, your journey. For the TV caller, feeling helpless and alone, the enlarged voice over the TV screen may represent the comfort of someone who cares. But it may also represent a false hope, a kind of long distance consolation without benefit of intimacy, trust, or one-on-one communication. Sometimes people may confide in others—family, friends, co-workers, even radio and TV personalities—and come away frustrated because they feel no better off than when they began. The person listening to them may be happy to listen, but unwilling or unable to commit to finding a solution.

- Can you recall a time when you were facing a serious problem and sought help from another? How did you feel?

____

____

____

____

- Can you recall a time when you felt let down by another's unwillingness to get involved? Why do you think it happened this way?

____

____

____

____

For a Christian, the easy answer to life's questions may be: "I know the way—Jesus." Indeed, a popular bumper sticker states, "If you are lost, I know the way." Jesus told his followers, "I am the way, and the truth, and the life." Yet for almost two thousand years, unraveling the meaning of this statement has not been a simple process. In fact, misunderstanding of Jesus as "the way" has led to diversity and sometimes hostility among church bodies that claim the name Christian. Sadly, ethnic or racial tension may exist in some parishes; some people may question one another's loyalty to "truth"; still others may attempt to judge the worth or "quality" of people's lives.

In addition to all you may have learned about Jesus and the Church as a community, it is also of great importance to think about who you are, individually, within the Church body. Your individuality is not something to be swallowed up by becoming Christian. The Church is not like a sponge that merely absorbed you. Rather, you now have the opportunity to assert your own individuality as you take your place alongside the already baptized.

You now have been united with the risen Christ in baptism. Christian belief over the ages has asserted that Jesus did not just die and live on only as a memory after the resurrection. On the contrary, this belief is that the risen Jesus is active in the lives of people of faith day after day, decade after decade, century after century. Indeed, Jesus promised to send the Holy Spirit to his disciples.

The Spirit of God may have moved you to inquire about baptism or may have sustained you through the calm and presence of others if you doubted your decision. You may have sensed the presence of the Spirit of God in the hospitality and welcome of your parish, or in the comfort felt in the response of others during a crisis or problem you faced. The key question, then, regarding your life in Christ may not be the standard one, "Who is Jesus?" Rather, it may be, "Who is Jesus for me?" It is this theme which you are invited to explore now.

EXPLORING THE SCRIPTURES

At one point in his public ministry, Jesus asked his disciples, "But who do you say that I am?" Peter said to him in reply, "You are the Messiah" (Mark 8:29). For your own response, search your heart and begin to think about who this Jesus is for you.

- How is Jesus your way?

____

____

____

____

- How is Jesus your truth?

____

____

____

____

- How is Jesus your life?

____

____

____

____

By completing the following statements, you may be better able to see what the theme of this chapter means to you. Your responses may also help you prepare for the scriptures that follow.

- A person who helps me keep going is ______________________

  ____

- I have learned much about the meaning of truth from ______________

  ____

- When it comes to really knowing how to live, I admire ______________

  because ______________________________________

  ____

The Scriptures of the Fifth Sunday of Easter

The readings of the fifth Sunday of the Easter season are from the Acts of the Apostles, the first letter of Peter, and the gospel according to John.

Acts of the Apostles 6:1–7

The story of the growth of the early Church is told, in part, in the Acts of the Apostles. The brief passage that follows tells about the selection of seven disciples to serve the new religious groups in Jerusalem. As you read the passage, think about what you consider when choosing someone to serve you, whether it be in political office, parish council service, or a local organization to which you belong.

In those days, as the number of disciples grew, the ones who spoke Greek complained that their widows were being neglected in the daily distribution of food, as compared with the widows of those who spoke Hebrew. The Twelve assembled the community of the disciples and said, "It is not right for us to neglect the word of God in order to wait on the tables. Look around among your own number, brothers, for seven men acknowledged to be deeply spiritual and prudent, and we shall appoint them to this task. This will permit us to concentrate on prayer and the ministry of the word." The proposal was unanimously accepted by the community. Following this they selected Stephen, a man filled with faith and a Holy Spirit; Philip, Prochorus, Nicanor, Timon, Parmenas and Nicolaus of Antioch, who had been a convert to Judaism. They presented these men to the apostles, who first prayed over them and then imposed hands on them.

The word of God continued to spread, while at the same time the number of the disciples in Jerusalem enormously increased. There were many priests among those who embraced the faith.

This passage reveals disagreement about practical issues among the early Christians. Greek-speaking and Aramaic-speaking Jews may be the two groups represented in the passage. In any case, the first followers of Jesus decide to gather the disciples and call for the selection of seven men to tend to the needs of Greek-speaking widows. The decision would also free the Twelve to devote themselves to spreading the word of God. One of the seven chosen, Stephen, is regarded as the first deacon and first martyr of the Church.

Think about how decisions are made in an organization of your choice: your parish, family, company, school, and so on. Focus on what, in your opinion, motivates people to decide what to do in making important decisions. The passage from Acts states that the disciples were to choose those who were "deeply spiritual and prudent."

What kinds of things are considered in making decisions in your organizations? What do you take into account when you have to make an important decision? The chart that follows may help you to explore decision-making in your life and in one or more organizations of your choice. Enter decisions made by you and by a group (or groups) to which you belong. Then tell why the decisions were made.

Exploring Decision–Making

	Decisions	*Why Made*
My Own Decisions		
Organization's Decisions		
Organization's Decisions		

Sometimes people develop a pattern or habit of making decisions. They may ignore new ideas that can affect a decision, choosing to do things the way they have always been done. A politician may remark, "I've voted the party line for 37 years, and there's no way I'll vote for any other party." Compare this attitude to the situation facing the first Christians. They could have relied on the existing ways of doing things and refused to deal with the situation as they did. However, the disciples were determined to ensure the spreading of the word of God along with providing for the needs of the community. The result? Growth in the ministry and life of the community.

Think again of some organizations that affect your life. Do you see a need for change? Is there resistance to change? Imagine what you would do if you could clarify matters. The following chart may help.

Organizations and Change

Organization	*Change Needed?*	*If I could, I would*
1.	Yes No	
2.	Yes No	
3.	Yes No	
4.	Yes No	

1 PETER 2:4–9

The young child methodically put together two dozen blocks to form a giant structure—perhaps the world's tallest, the child imagined. Reds, yellows, blues, greens—the brightly colored blocks, now precariously balanced atop and alongside one another, formed a marvelous sight. But the building was not to remain long, for the child imagined an even greater masterpiece. Slowly the youngster pulled out the red block at the base of the structure—the cornerstone, as it were. The blocks tumbled to the floor, to the gleeful delight of the young builder, who began again, laying one block atop another, but always beginning at the corner.

This second reading gives you the opportunity to think about how you relate to the cornerstone of the Christian faith, Jesus Christ. As you read the passage, think about why you believe in Jesus and how you are a "living stone."

Come to the Lord, a living stone, rejected by men but approved, nonetheless, and precious in God's eyes. You too are living stones, built as an edifice of spirit, into a holy priesthood, offering spiritual sacrifices acceptable to God through Jesus Christ. For Scripture has it:
"See, I am laying a cornerstone in Zion,
an approved stone, and precious.
He who puts his faith in it shall not be shaken."

The stone is of value for you who have faith.
For those without faith, it is rather,
"A stone which the builders rejected
that became a cornerstone."

It is likewise "an obstacle and a stumbling stone." Those who stumble and fall are the disbelievers in God's word; it belongs to their destiny to do so.

You, however, are "a chosen race, a royal priesthood, a consecrated nation, a people he claims for his own to proclaim the glorious works" of the One who called you from darkness into his marvelous light.

In this passage Christ is characterized as the cornerstone of Christian faith. The symbolism of the stone is not a creation of the author of 1 Peter. The author draws from Old Testament notions—Isaiah 28:16 and Psalm 118:22—to lay the claim that Jesus is the living stone from which the believer draws life. For persons of faith in Jesus, the stone called Christ is more than just another lifeless or immovable object, weighed down by its own mass. It is the source and foundation of life, linking believers not only to Christ but to one another. For those who reject Christ, the stone may be a puzzle and question mark in the story of life.

Look at the picture of the building that follows. Each piece of wood is linked to another. One board either supports or is supported by another, and the removal of one may cause the others to sag. There is something mutual going on here; no board stands alone, and the nails do not enter a board and pop through the other side. They hold one another together, finally forming a structure that, hopefully, can withstand whatever may threaten to bring them down. The boards draw support from the lowest members which serve as a foundation to the whole structure. If a corner were removed, the entire building would collapse or, at least, sag. The support of the cornerstone of the building is not just upward, to the boards above it, but outward, to those around it. One could also say it is downward, too, since without such support, the structure could come crashing down.

For a baptized person, like you, the cornerstone of faith is Jesus Christ. For a Christian, Jesus is the living stone whom death could not conquer.

- Think about how you relate to Jesus. Think about what it is that enables you to believe in him. Think, too, of times you have felt his comfort, his peace. Ask yourself: In what situation recently have you experienced Jesus as cornerstone?

Sometimes Christians unintentionally forget about what they are called to become. They forget that they are linked to the cornerstone of faith by their becoming living stones—people and communities of faith who act on their belief in Christ by being open to the Spirit of God in their lives.

Now consider how you are a living stone. You may have a new insight into the way you relate to another person. You may assist in resolving a personal problem of a friend of yours. Or you may sense the need for healing in your family or marriage, or a work or social relationship. Whatever the situation, you are called to share the life that is yours as best you can. When you do this, you are being a living stone.

Close your eyes and relax your senses. Clear your head of thoughts and distractions. After you open your eyes, try to decide on one specific thing you will do this week for another person. Use the space below if you wish to jot down some ideas.

JOHN 14:1–12

Sometimes people feel terribly alone: the person who has just lost a job, the couple whose baby is seriously ill, the family suffering with a loved one with Alzheimer's disease. All need reassurance that the situation is somehow manageable, no matter how hopeless it may seem. Trusting in Jesus may help with such struggles. As you read the passage that follows, think of times in your life when you needed to be reassured.

Jesus said to his disciples:
"Do not let your hearts be troubled.
Have faith in God
and faith in me.
In my Father's house there are many dwelling places;
otherwise, how could I have told you
that I was going to prepare a place for you?
I am indeed going to prepare a place for you,
and then I shall come back to take you with me,
that where I am you also may be.
You know the way that leads where I go."
"Lord," said Thomas, "we do not know where you are going. How can we know the way?" Jesus told him:
"I am the way, and the truth, and the life; no one comes to the Father but through me.
If you really knew me, you would know my Father also.
From this point on you know him; you have seen him."
"Lord," Philip said to him, "show us the Father and that will be enough for us." "Philip," Jesus replied, "after I have been with you all this time, you still do not know me?
"Whoever has seen me has seen the Father.
How can you say, 'Show us the Father'?
Do you not believe that I am in the Father
and the Father is in me?
The words I speak are not spoken of myself;
it is the Father who lives in me accomplishing his works.
Believe me that I am in the Father
and the Father is in me,
or else, believe because of the works I do.

I solemnly assure you,
the man who has faith in me
will do the works I do, and greater far than these.
Why? Because I go to the Father."

This passage begins Jesus' last discourse to his disciples before his death. It is considered by some to be one of the most beautiful addresses in all the scriptures. Jesus' reassuring words that begin this discourse are a "calm down" message to his disciples: "Do not let your hearts be troubled. Have faith in God and faith in me." The disciples are troubled by Jesus' pending separation from them; he says to Peter: "Where I am going, you cannot follow me now, though you will follow later" (John 13:36). Jesus urges his disciples to maintain trust in him. One senses that Jesus is trying to help them put together pieces of a complex puzzle. To the quizzical Thomas, Jesus replies, "I am the way, and the truth, and the life."

The preceding "I am . . ." statement of Jesus is one of a number of such statements recorded in John's gospel. Each of them provides a clue to Jesus' identity. Jesus tries to help his followers come to see not only who he is but also what they are called to become.

Jesus is the way—he is not the one who just shows the way of freedom, but is freedom itself. In Jesus a Christian finds salvation. Jesus is the truth—not only a great prophet telling the truth about God's love for people, but the living truth of who God is. Jesus is also the life—again, not some great preacher who only sets out rules and norms, but in him there is life itself. Jesus and his Father are one. Jesus is the way to the God of all truth, the source of all life.

Jesus may have felt amazed after hearing Philip say to him, "Lord, show us the Father and that will be enough for us." Jesus responds as if to say, "Come on, Philip, wise up! We've been together for three years, and you still can't see what's going on? What must I do?"

Of course, Philip and the other disciples are fearing the worst. They do not want Jesus to leave them. They fail to understand all that is happening around them. William Barclay points out that "in a very short time life for the disciples was going to fall in. Their world was going to collapse in chaos around them. At such a time there was only one thing to do—stubbornly to hold on to trust in God."[1] Certainly, people today can identify with such a scenario. Perhaps you were confused before your baptism; you may have doubted your decision or wondered if Jesus really is the Son of God.

Conversion to Christ is not an automatic type of thing: press a button, and out comes a convert! That would reduce the water rite of baptism to no more than magic. Conversion takes a lifetime; it is an ongoing coming to live the hope of the risen Lord. It is a process of coming to see Jesus as one's way, truth, and life. With Christ as the cornerstone, with one's parish as "builders," one may be able to face life's fears and challenges with renewed hope and confidence.

- Suppose someone were to say to you, "I've given my life to Jesus. That's all one has to do. Then all problems go away." How would you respond?

____

____

____

____

For the couple whose baby is ill, for the jobless person, for the family suffering with an Alzheimer's patient—for all these and more, the challenge is to trust in God, in oneself, and in the willingness of others to provide support and hope. With such help, a person may begin to feel confident in finding that crises do not have to be faced alone, but with others who are Christ to them.

- Think about a time of crisis in your life. Who supported and reassured you?

____

____

____

____

- How can you reassure others now?

____

____

____

____

RENEWING YOUR LIFE OF FAITH

As you explore who Jesus is for you and renew your life of faith, you are again invited to think back to the liturgy of your baptism. There is more to be explored about your becoming Christian. For a baptized person, like you, the eucharist can become the ongoing source of a way of life. This way of life is grounded in the truth that the Spirit of God is present in one's life.

Jesus' statement that he is way, truth, and life can give new meaning to how you choose to live. For example, gathering with others for worship can become more than maintaining a weekly practice that may have become routine. Deciding to be baptized can mean more than wanting to join a certain parish. For a catechumen, attending preparation sessions can become more than wanting a night out. These experiences or decisions can lead to deeper, stronger meanings that enable the baptized person, like you, to act on one's belief. Gathering for the eucharistic liturgy just might develop into an awareness of what it means to worship with others, and draw or give support from or to them for the week to come. The sacrament of the Lord's body and blood may result in transforming Christians into a united community called "Church." Deciding to join a particular local church may lead to becoming an active member of the parish. Participating in a parish session or event may become a recognition of a responsibility to investigate what all this teaching really can mean for you.

For one newly baptized person, returning to her parish church and seeing the variety of hanging banners and the messages on them is an important reminder of her experience of becoming Christian:

> In Advent it's "Receive your new way of life." To me that was really symbolic because this was my first step. And it was saying to me, "This is your new life, and you're going to be a part of us." Then for Lent it's "Accept your new way of life" and I was ready to accept it and I wanted to, and that had a lot of meaning to me. I know they did it for everybody, but I felt like they put it up for us, or for me.... Banners go from "receive" to "accept" to "live." So you're starting the process, and then you're getting involved in it, and then you're living it.

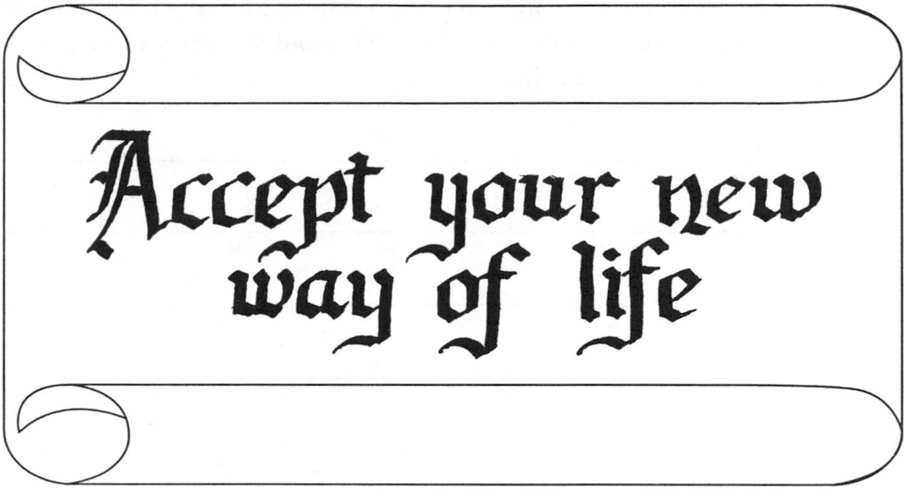

Accept your new way of life

To live
is Christ,
to die
is gain

- Imagine you are asked to sponsor a person who is thinking about joining the Church. What would you say to the inquirer about the effect of your decision to become Christian on your life?

____

____

____

____

The Eucharist: Life and Liturgy

One of the sources of continuing to develop a life of faith is your regular celebration of the eucharist. The *Rite of Christian Initiation of Adults* points out that "sharing in the eucharist" (#244)[2] is an essential part of life after baptism. The eucharist is the one sacrament of initiation that you are called to celebrate over and over again. You were baptized and confirmed once, leading to the first of what will hopefully be many occasions to participate in the sacrificial meal of Jesus Christ. Catholics believe that it is a sacred meal through which all assembled are somehow united in faith, transformed by the body and blood of Jesus Christ.

In the eucharist, a Christian celebrates the mysterious belief in God's gift of Jesus really present in the simple symbols of bread and wine, now become his body and blood. In the fourth century, Theodore of Mopsuestia would call these symbols "the food and the drink which keep us alive in this world."[3] The nourishment of the eucharist at mass is food for life after baptism. The diagram that follows puts this statement in visual form:

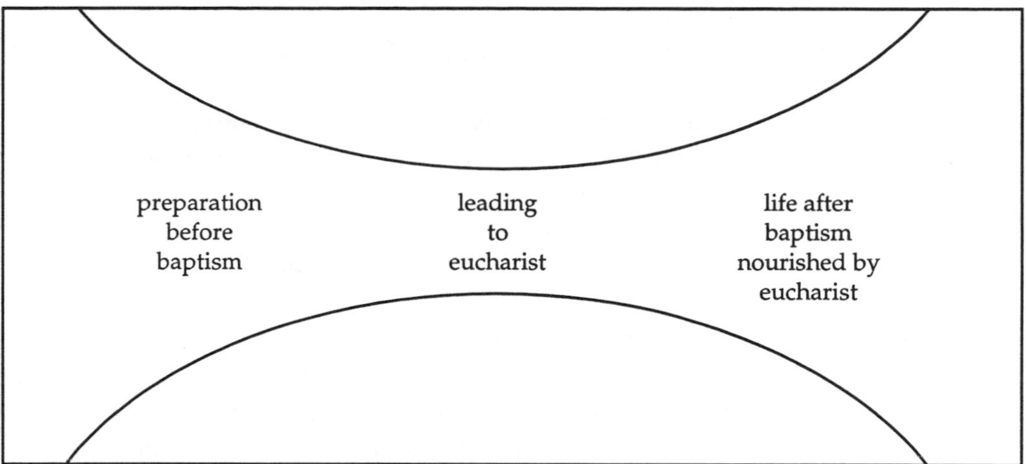

To say that the eucharist is to be the nourishment for the baptized is not intended as a statement somehow divorced from what some might call "real life." In other words, the eucharist is food for broken lives, hopeful lives, shaken lives, trusting lives, and saddened lives.

Each time you gather for the celebration of the eucharist, passages from the scriptures are proclaimed. There has been a section on exploring the scriptures in each chapter of this book. Indeed, each of these chapters has been a type of "liturgy of the word," encouraging you to listen in the quiet of your heart to the word of God and call of Christ.

What is it about the mass that makes it so central to one's ongoing life as a Christian? To answer this question, it would be good to focus on your experience of the liturgy of the eucharist. You are, in a way, not only thinking back to your first celebration of this sacrament, but are also looking at what hopefully has become a weekly experience of prayer and worship in this sacred memorial.

You probably took your place alongside others from your parish for your first celebration of eucharist. Having been baptized and confirmed in the Spirit, you participated in this shared prayer of the Church for the first time. Perhaps you were asked to bring the gifts of bread and wine to the presider, who said this prayer over them:

Lord,
accept the prayers and offerings of your people.
With your help
may this Easter mystery of our redemption
bring to perfection the saving work you have
begun in us.

We ask this through Christ our Lord.[4]

You may have responded Amen to the prayer, and the liturgy continued. You may not, however, have been aware of all that was happening around you. Perhaps you were so moved by your experience of baptism that this climax of the eucharist somehow escaped you. That is one reason why it is important to begin to review it here.

The priest asked that all assembled lift their hearts up to the Lord in praise and thanksgiving. He did not say "open your ears" or "listen carefully," but "lift up your hearts."[5] One is reminded of the words of Cyril of Jerusalem to the newly baptized during his fourth-century Easter week preaching on the eucharist. Cyril, in referring to the introduction to the eucharistic prayer, said:

> Then the celebrant cries: "Lift up your hearts." For truly it is right in that most awful hour to have one's heart on high with God, not below, occupied with earth and the things of earth. In effect, then, the bishop commands everyone to banish worldly thoughts and workaday cares and to have their hearts in heaven with the good God.
>
> Assenting, you answer, "We have them lifted up to the Lord." ... At all times we should commemorate God, but at least, if this is not possible to human weakness, we must aspire to it in that hour.[6]

Mind and heart were to be one in the conclusive part of the Easter liturgy, just as they had been one in the celebration of baptism. You may recall your feelings during the moments between your baptism and the eucharistic part of the celebration. Perhaps it struck you that you would never be baptized again, but could always share in the eucharist over and over again. You may have felt happy and thankful not to have to leave the church after the readings as may have happened all during the catechumenate.

The liturgy continued with the prayer of thanks to God, proclaiming God's glory and offering him praise. The prayer ended with the assembly joining together to sing of the holiness of God:

> Holy, holy, holy Lord, God of power and might,
> heaven and earth are full of your glory.
> Hosanna in the highest.
> Blessed is he who comes in the name of the Lord.
> Hosanna in the highest.[7]

Although this prayer is obviously one of praise to God, it is also a powerful reminder of the joy of those who hold fast to the loving God. In the eucharist Christians offer thanks for God's blessings, the greatest of which is Jesus—the way, the truth, and the life.

- Is there a particular part of the liturgy that helps you to focus on:

  — Jesus as your way, truth, and life?

  — the blessings and wonder of God?

____

____

____

____

When viewing television, listening to the radio, or reading the newspaper this week, try to pick up signals of what people hold as their way, truth, and life. This is really a way of getting at what they value. Examine what they seem to value, using the following checklist as a guide. Add other items to the list if you wish.

Checklist of Values

_____ independence	_____ friendship
_____ prestige	_____ money
_____ concern for others	_____ acceptance
_____ security	_____ freedom
_____ achievement	_____ hope
______________________	______________________

After doing the above, look over the list for yourself, noting what you value. Then complete these statements.

- I expected others to ____

  ____

  ____

- I was surprised that I value ________________________________

  because ______________________________________

  ____

The eucharist is food for the way you have chosen to live as a follower of Jesus. You have your own way of living as a Christian. No one, really, can duplicate how you decide to live or how you express what you value. You are able to create an individual response to Jesus in the eucharist. As St. Paul says, "There are different kinds of spiritual gifts but the same Spirit; there are different forms of service but the same Lord; there are different workings but the same God who produces all of them in everyone" (1 Corinthians 12:4–6).

Did You Know?

The relation between baptism and eucharist has been mentioned periodically throughout this book. Theodore of Mopsuestia, speaking in the fourth century, put well the link between these two sacraments. He told newly baptized Christians:

> In this world we owe our existence to two things, birth and nourishment; we derive our existence from our birth, but in order to continue in existence we need nourishment, and without it birth is inevitably followed by decay. In the world to come we likewise derive our existence from our birth and resurrection; but since we are immortal our existence will be permanent. . . .
>
> Since we are born now at baptism symbolically and by signs, we need also to receive under the same symbols nourishment which is in keeping with the new life we receive at baptism, and which will enable us to preserve this life.[8]

Theodore's use of such terms as birth and nourishment may enable you to think about your own experience of these sacraments of initiation. However, Theodore's stress on "the world to come" might tempt a Christian to bypass present-day needs and concerns. Chapter 3 gave examples of hunger and invited you to think about eucharist in relation to hungers in your life and in the world. Think again about hungers now, and about what nourishment may be needed to satisfy them. The sentences that follow may help you do this.

- I am now experiencing a hunger for ______________________________

  ____

  ____

- A hunger my parish or other organization is experiencing now is ________

____

____

- What might you do to relieve these hungers?

____

____

____

____

Obviously, for Theodore, the eucharist was to be the source of nourishment for a Christian after baptism. It is not enough to be born—what baby can fend for itself after birth? What if the baby were left to survive without the loving arms of a mother or father, and without the nourishment born of the mother's body? The consequences could be tragic. Similarly, it is one thing for a Christian to declare at one's baptism, "Jesus is my life." But to say in the days, weeks, and years after baptism, "I cannot live without Jesus," is another matter. For such a person the eucharist may become food for a way of life united with others in the body of Christ, the Church.

- During the coming week, ask two or three people why they worship, or "go to church." Then think about what motivates you to worship. You may want to use the space below to make some notes.

____

____

____

____

ACCEPTING THE CHALLENGE

Sometimes people get confused between what they are told is *the* way to follow Jesus and the best way for them to follow Jesus. There may be a difference between knowing the way of Jesus as you may have learned about it and choosing the best way for you to live as a Christian. One person's way may not be possible or beneficial for another. People may find different means of expressing their belief in and acceptance of Jesus for their lives.

You can get confused if you try to imitate others and find yourself unable to accomplish what you set out to do. For example, a parishioner you know may have a great ability for working with young people or be just the right person for coordinating parish human service programs. You, on the other hand, may feel uncertain about participating in either of these ministries. Instead of talking yourself into trying to be like someone else, it might be more productive to explore your own gifts and abilities and how you might use them in your parish. In the space below, indicate three good qualities about yourself. Please don't be shy. Instead, focus on those qualities that make you the person you are.

Something Good about Me

1. ______________________________

2. ______________________________

3. ______________________________

- Is there some way any of these qualities can be used to the benefit of your parish? Complete the sentences to help you decide.

- I believe that my quality of ______________________________

  could enable me to ______________________________

  ____

- This is because I really believe that I ______________________________

  ____

  ____

Looking Back

Throughout this chapter, the theme has been Jesus as way, truth, and life. However, one might conclude that growth in faith happens in seclusion, in a manner that distances one from other people. One may want to visualize such a simple approach with either of these diagrams:

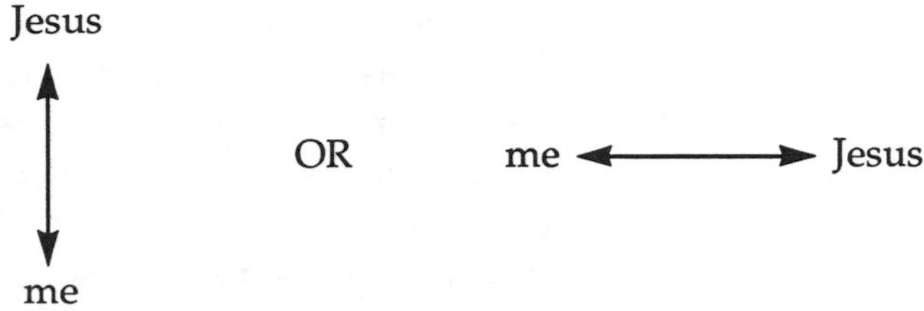

What if the vision just presented were broadened? What if seeing Jesus as way, truth, and life were represented with relationships with others as central to what it means to live in Christ? The drawing might then look like this:

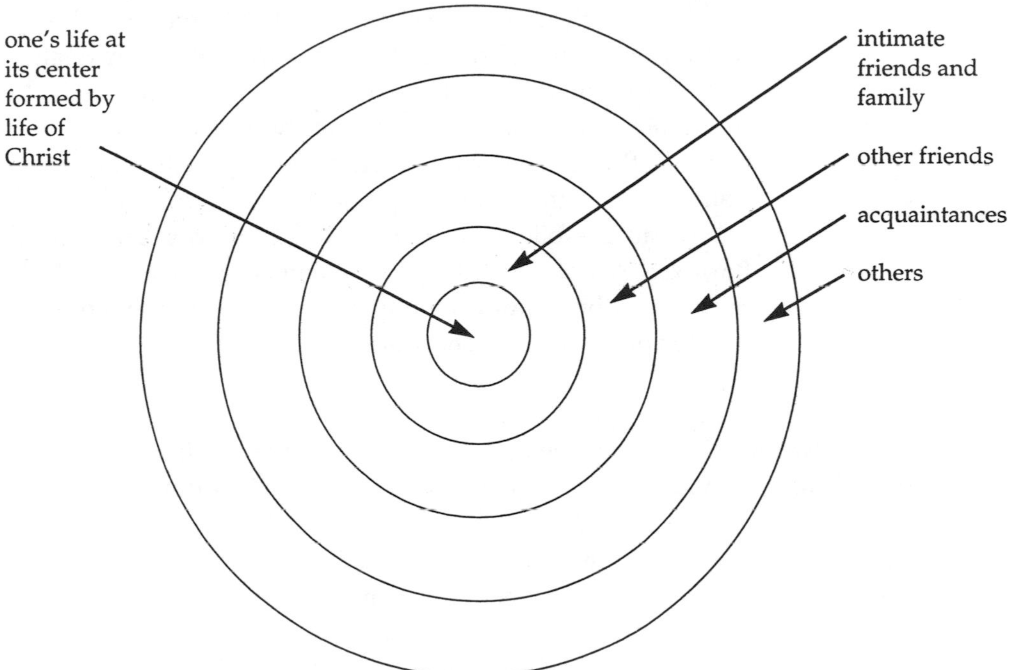

Each ring is a set of relationships with people you know, and the center of life is one's own life formed by the life of Christ. In this view, the way a Christian relates to others is shaped and enriched by one's relationship with Christ. Way, truth, and life begin to take on meanings perhaps never thought of before, as a believer begins to explore the impact of one's faith in Christ on how one relates to others. To help you understand this, read the following example.

Many Christians worship for one hour on weekends. They are motivated by as many reasons as there are people. One person might worship to seek strength from God, another to hear a favorite homilist, another to satisfy Church law. But another reason for worshiping is to gather in fellowship with others. After all, if a Christian, like you, claims Jesus as one's way, why not worship with people you have journeyed with along the way? If Jesus is the truth, who is it who has helped you to see this truth? If Jesus is the life, what lives of others have been examples to you of this teaching? In other words, a newly baptized person is not only welcomed into a relationship with Christ, but is welcomed through relationships with others. Your baptism did not occur privately, but in the presence of the parish assembly. The local community of faith, the Church, had an important part to play before your baptism, and its ongoing role is no less important now.

Read the following words of Cyril of Jerusalem to newly baptized people. See if you can detect the truth of Cyril's message as he examines the way Christians are called to live before approaching the eucharist.

> Next the deacon cries: "Welcome one another," and "Let us kiss one another." You must not suppose that this kiss is the kiss customarily exchanged in the streets by ordinary friends. This kiss is different, effecting, as it does, a commingling of souls and mutually pledging unreserved forgiveness. The kiss, then, is a sign of a true union of hearts, banishing every grudge. It was this that Christ had in view when he said: "If, when you are bringing your gift to the altar, you suddenly remember that your brother has a grievance against you, leave your offering by the altar; first go and make your peace with your brother, and then come back and offer your gift."[9]

This passage may help you to see how your relationships with others affect how you relate to Jesus. This is important to think about before you depart from home for mass on Sunday. Your own sign of peace during the Sunday celebration of eucharist can become a joyful expression of happiness, hope, and healing within your family or parish. Ask yourself:

- Do I need to offer someone forgiveness? Will I?

____

____

____

____

- How might I be more charitable or less critical this week at work or at home? Will I try?

____

____

____

____

Review briefly the sections on exploring the scriptures (pages 150-161) and renewing your life of faith (pages 161-170). Perhaps something you read particularly interested you. This type of review can help you to sharpen what it means for you to say that Jesus is your way, truth, and life.

For the scripture readings in this chapter, complete the following.

- Acts of the Apostles 6:1–7—A role I see myself having in my parish five years from now is . . .

____

____

____

____

- 1 Peter 2:4–9—Look at the last verse of this reading. What is the first word that comes to mind when you see the phrase "darkness into . . . light"?

____

____

____

____

- John 14:1–12—Jesus has said that the one "who has faith in me will do the works I do, and greater far than these." Imagine for a moment that the future of the world is in your hands. The only limitation you have is that you are not permitted to use words to achieve whatever goal you set for yourself. What gesture(s) would you use? Why?

____

____

____

____

For the section on renewing your life of faith (pages 161-170), recall what was said about the eucharist as the source of nourishment for a Christian after baptism. In a sense, all that you do during the week leads up to the celebration of eucharist on the weekend. Indeed, many newly baptized people have described their experience of preparing for eucharist this way. The other side of eucharist is the side that leads you from the celebration, to live as a Christian in the days that follow.

Select one or more situations from your weekly routine—for example, reading, attending a meeting, viewing television, and so on. For one of them, ask yourself:

- Does ______________________________ have anything to do with eucharist for me? How? If not, what will I do about it?

  ____

  ____

  ____

  ____

- How can I nourish others' lives? Will I?

  ____

  ____

  ____

  ____

You are at the conclusion of this fifth chapter. You have explored a variety of themes so far:

- the challenge of your life of faith
- your new life of faith
- the center of your life of faith
- the fullness of your life of faith
- the way, truth, and life of faith

The flow of the first four chapters relates well to the focus of this chapter: your development as a person whose life is rooted in Jesus, the way, the truth, and the life. As you continue to live as a baptized Christian, be confident in your ability to live as a disciple of Jesus. Remember these words of Ambrose of Milan to the newly baptized: "What the mouth speaks, let the mind within confess; what words utter, let the heart feel."[10]

6

The Spirit of Your Life of Faith

PSALM–PRAYER

Shout joyfully to God, all you on earth;
    sing of his glorious name;
    give him glorious praise.
Say to God: "How awesome your deeds! . . .
All on earth fall in worship before you;
    they sing of you, sing of your name!"

Come and see the works of God,
    awesome in the deeds done for us.
He changed the sea to dry land;
    through the river they passed on foot.
Therefore let us rejoice in him,
    who rules by might forever, . . .

Come and hear, all you who fear God,
    while I recount what has been done for me. . . .
Blessed be God, who did not refuse me
    the kindness I sought in prayer.

Psalm 66: 1–7, 16, 20

Overview

"That's the spirit!"
"Put some life into it!"
"Give it all you've got!"

When spoken, these remarks urge people to press onward, to move ahead. One struggling to keep his or her head above water may find the inner resourcefulness to keep on going.

This chapter has to do with what urges and moves a newly baptized person, like you, to continue to explore what it is to be a Christian. This life-source is God the Holy Spirit—the Spirit of your life of faith. The chapter also encourages you to explore further your ongoing experience of the eucharist with your parish. You may experience an urging of the Spirit from deep within yourself to gather with others for worship and to look at your own life, nourished by eucharist, as a source of hope, strength, and life to others.

Take your time with this chapter. Perhaps discussing parts of it with family, friends, or a godparent may give you new insights into why you believe what you believe.

EXPLORING YOUR EXPERIENCE

When people make a decision to do or not to do something, they may experience a variety of steps in coming to the decision. They may, without even realizing it:

- determine factors affecting the decision
- assess the importance of each of the factors
- reduce the number of factors to those that are considered important
- consider possible consequences
- make the decision

Consciously or unconsciously, you may have followed this type of approach in reaching your decision to investigate membership in the Church. One newly baptized person, in reaching a decision to be baptized, explored her motivation for seeking baptism this way. In recalling a conversation she had had with her fiance, she noted: "I had told him that I wanted to become a Catholic not because he was one but because I wanted to do it for myself."

For a Christian, one factor to consider in seeking baptism is the role of the Holy Spirit, the third Person of the Holy Trinity. To many, the Spirit is some mysterious comforter, and not quite understandable. Still, the Spirit of God is considered by Christians to be somehow a part of coming to experience the love of God and to developing faith in God. The *Rite of Christian Initiation of Adults* (#1) speaks of the Holy Spirit who opens the hearts of persons seeking baptism. One might say that the Holy Spirit is that living presence of God moving people to heal, to love, and to care for one another. Somehow, the Spirit penetrates people's lives, urging them to live in faith and decide to do what they believe is best for them.

The Presence of God

The following groups of statements are from two different sources: remarks of newly baptized Christians, and remarks of two fourth-century preachers, John Chrysostom (for Groups One and Two) and Cyril of Jerusalem (Group Three). As you read each pair, think about the presence of the Spirit in your life and what the Spirit has meant for you as a newly baptized person.

GROUP ONE

> I always was raised without any religion and from the time I was in the first grade I just always had this desire.... I'd always find myself talking to God.

Therefore, you who are coming to God, first believe in God and then speak out that word loud and clear. For if you cannot do this, you will be able neither to speak nor understand any other. Let me pass over that mysterious birth which has no human witnesses. Let me bring before you that birth which took place here below and was witnessed by many. Through this very explanation I shall secure your faith in things, because without faith you would never be able to accept it.[1]

GROUP TWO

> I know it's not the actual church that makes the church but . . . it's the feeling . . . I'm sure the concrete affects it . . . but when you go in it's the people you have a feeling about. . . . During the peace offering or whatever people will really go out of their way. To reach over, cross an aisle or whatever.

When we are about to participate in the sacred Table, we are also instructed to offer a holy greeting.... Our gathering becomes like the gathering of the apostles when, because all believed, there was one heart and one soul.

Bound together in this fashion, we ought to approach the sacred mysteries. Hear what Christ says: If thou art offering thy gift at the altar, and there rememberest that thy brother has anything against thee, go first to be reconciled to thy brother and then offer thy gift. He did not say: "First offer"; He said: First be reconciled and then offer. When the gift is set before us, let us, therefore, first become reconciled with one another and then proceed to the sacrifice.[2]

GROUP THREE

> I felt that the *RCIA* program was terrific. It starts off slowly but surely and makes everyone feel comfortable. It was very easy to get into prayer. ...My hopes were that I would fit in....I really knew nothing about Church and God. But I learned Church is made up of very friendly people.

For whatever the Holy Spirit touches is hallowed and changed.[3]

Exploring the dynamics of your inner striving and yearning may help you to focus on what you are all about. It may help you to discover what keeps you going: goals, friends, faith, God, and so on.

Journey and conversion are two words that have already appeared in your book. Often, these words are used along with commentary on the Holy Spirit to provide a deeper sense of God's presence during one's lifetime.

- What kept you going during your preparation for baptism?

____

____

____

____

- Do you recall some concrete experience of God within you? What was it? Do you believe the Spirit of God is with you now? Why is that?

____

____

____

____

Judging from interviews with newly baptized persons, like yourself, it is not unusual to uncover a sense of God's presence as the individual discusses what lies at the heart of his or her life of faith. Was that true for what you just wrote?

EXPLORING THE SCRIPTURES

The main focus of this chapter is on the Spirit of your life of faith. With this in mind, read the following verses slowly and purposefully.

> The spirit of the LORD shall rest upon him (Isaiah 11:2).

> The spirit of the Lord GOD is upon me,
> because the LORD has anointed me
> (Isaiah 61:1).

> I will give you a new heart and place a new spirit within you (Ezekiel 36:26).

> Then afterward I will pour out
> my spirit upon all mankind (Joel 3:1).

These scripture verses are all from the Old Testament. They are listed here for two reasons: to help you explore the close union of the Spirit of God with the chosen people; and to remind you that, despite the fact that the readings for the sixth Sunday of Easter are from the New Testament, the Spirit of God was active in giving life to people from the dawn of creation.

God's Spirit may be characterized as so vast that any description is light years from being adequate. From the Bible, one may come to an understanding of the Spirit of God. The Church reminds us of the Spirit's movement among us, prompting our faithful response to God's call in our lives. Another source for exploring the Spirit of God is people's own experiences of life. Oftentimes, there are peak moments in life: times of birth and death; injury and healing; despair and hope. The following passage tells of one such experience. It is excerpted from a diary entry of a young man who had just buried a close relative. As you read the excerpt, see if you can detect in the writer's attitude of faith a confidence in the presence of God in the situation described.

> Dear Diary,
>
> A dear and close relative, this Aunt Estelle. Her remarkable faith and persistent goodness stayed with her right to the end. As I helped make funeral arrangements I thought about the meaning of life. I sensed Estelle's satisfaction at conquering death and being one with God. I experienced a certainty about what is to come. (After all, I thought, how could anyone like Estelle deserve or receive anything less?)
>
> I was moved to reflect on this woman's simple yet powerful faith. She had endured six years of suffering, with pain to the end. How did she do it? Why did she suffer? She was an extremely charitable person—always giving, always pleased with whatever she received.
>
> Jesus was so present in this situation. I knew he was with us, and I knew he was with Estelle.

> Jesus was our strength in loss, our hope in need. Somehow, our family really pulled together during this time. Somehow we were one, especially in our sharing together the eucharist at Estelle's funeral. I felt that somehow her spirit endured, and I felt this so strongly for myself when I took the eucharist in my hands.[4]

In this chapter you can explore the Spirit in your life as well as your ongoing celebration of the eucharist. As you read the scriptures that follow, see if there is for you more than one way of understanding the Spirit of God. Perhaps you will be able to understand better your own ideas of the Spirit and the action of the Spirit in your life.

The Scriptures of the Sixth Sunday of Easter

The scriptures for this Sunday all refer to the Holy Spirit. The first two readings are from the Acts of the Apostles and the first letter of Peter, respectively. The gospel is that of John.

In the chart that follows, enter the first four words that come to mind when you think of the Holy Spirit in your life. After reading the passages, see if there are other words you would add to your list. This exercise may enable you to strengthen your awareness of how you understand the Spirit of God in your life.

Holy Spirit Word List "A"

Before Reading Passages

1. ____________________ 3. ____________________

2. ____________________ 4. ____________________

ACTS OF THE APOSTLES 8:5–8, 14–17

This reading is from that part of the Acts of the Apostles that describes the story of how the gospel message about Jesus was preached through Judea and Samaria. It tells of the work of Philip and of his journey from Jerusalem to Samaria to preach the word of God. (See Acts 6:1–7.) As you read the passage, think of what you do to let others know of how you feel about being baptized. You might ask yourself:

- Do I feel a responsibility to let others know of what faith means to me?

____

____

____

____

Philip went down to the town of Samaria and there proclaimed the Messiah. Without exception, the crowds that heard Philip and saw the miracles he performed attended closely to what he had to say. There were many who had unclean spirits, which came out shrieking loudly. Many others were paralytics or cripples, and these were cured. The rejoicing in that town rose to fever pitch.

When the apostles in Jerusalem heard that Samaria had accepted the word of God, they sent Peter and John to them. The two went down to these people and prayed that they might receive the Holy Spirit. It had not as yet come down upon any of them since they had only been baptized in the name of the Lord Jesus. The pair upon arriving imposed hands on them and they received the Holy Spirit.

This passage demonstrates the link between the baptism of the Samaritans and the completion of their baptism by the laying on of hands by the apostles Peter and John. People in the town of Samaria responded to Philip's preaching, but their response could not be complete without the imposition of hands, a sign of the gift of the Holy Spirit in their lives.

The laying on of hands was not a new creation of Christianity. Thomas Marsh points out that "imposition of hands was an established Jewish rite expressing participation in the spirit of the community, in this case the presence of the Spirit of God."[5]

A Christian may believe that the Spirit of God acts in ways unknown and mysterious to humanity. However, it is not unreasonable to expect believers to see the power of the Spirit in their own selves and the goodness of their own lives. For some, this involves taking a risk—perhaps like Philip in the passage from Acts, and seeking to alert others to the saving goodness of Jesus Christ.

- Do you have any ideas about how Christians might work together more effectively?

____

____

____

____

- Who or what might encourage you to be more of a risk-taker in living your faith?

____

____

____

____

1 PETER 3:15–18

Too hasty a reading of this passage could result in one's condemning "this" life for the sake of the life to come. One may wonder why such issues as uneasiness over international weapons distribution or world hunger are worth worrying about, if all that matters is "the realm of the spirit." As you read, think of your life now as the life of the spirit, and of how you are a source of hope for persons who are in need—whether it be physical, spiritual, emotional, or otherwise.

Venerate the Lord, that is, Christ, in your hearts. Should anyone ask you the reason for this hope of yours be ever ready to reply, but speak gently and respectfully. Keep your conscience clear so that, whenever you are defamed, those who libel your way of life in Christ may be disappointed. If it should be God's will that you suffer, it is better to do so for good deeds than for evil ones.

This is why Christ died for sins once for all, a just man for the sake of the unjust: so that he could lead you to God. He was put to death insofar as fleshly existence goes, but was given life in the realm of the spirit.

Peter urges followers of Christ to accept criticism "gently and respectfully." They are to remember that the source of their way of life is Christ, the risen Lord, present in the realm of the spirit. Peter points out that the realm of the spirit is the realm of life with God.

One phrase that may go unnoticed in this passage is this one: "So that he could lead you to God." A Christian might too quickly assume that leading others to God is only the work of Christ. In other words, one may be tempted to sit back and live without concern for the impact one's life may have on leading others to God.

Think of who it was who led you to God while you were a catechumen. Was it only your own response to Christ? Was it also persons you met along the way and have been influenced by all during your life? Parish communities, catechumenate teams, and sponsors especially, are asked to help catechumens prepare for baptism. However, one may sometimes forget about people or events that lead to serious reflection on the ultimate meaning in life, which is called "God" by many people in the world. For example, one person may sense in the death of a close friend that somehow life has been changed but not snuffed out. Another may be overwhelmed by the care and concern of someone loved, and be unable to express in words the love he or she feels. Still another may be inspired by the fortitude of a Bob Wieland, the Vietnam veteran who completed a New York marathon despite the fact he lost both his legs during the Vietnam War.

- Try to identify in the space that follows an event, individual, or community that has led you to God. Why do you think there was such an effect on you?

Moving Toward God

Person/Event/Community	*Affected Me Because*

As a newly baptized person, you may find that trying to convince others of what you believe may not be the best way to live according to your beliefs. Others may be influenced not only by what you think but also by who you are. The way you live and relate to others may have a great impact on how others and you come to God. The question for the believer is not "How can I get others to be just like me?" but "How can I live in line with my beliefs, sharing this faith which is God's gift to me?"

How might a Christian, like you, live as you believe? The list below contains some responses to this question. Check those that you agree with and add others if you wish.

Living by My Beliefs

_____ positive, hopeful attitude toward life

_____ struggle on behalf of others

_____ admitting when I'm at fault

_____ standing up for what I believe in

_____ being open to others' disagreements with me

_____ trying to "live and let live"

_____ ____

_____ ____

_____ ____

Your living by one or more of the responses above may result in others inquiring about why you are a Christian. Decide now to think about your choice(s) during the coming week to help you focus on why you believe what you believe. Be open to the realm of the spirit, so that you may "venerate the Lord, that is, Christ, in your heart."

JOHN 14:15–21

This passage begins Jesus' last address to his disciples before his death. You may notice that the first and last verses of the passage include Jesus' use of the word love. He seems intent on assuring his followers of his presence with them always. As you read the passage, think about someone you love and how you show your love for him or her.

Jesus said to his disciples:
"If you love me
and obey the commands I give you,
I will ask the Father
and he will give you another Paraclete—
to be with you always:
the Spirit of truth,
whom the world cannot accept,
since it neither sees him nor recognizes him;
but you can recognize him
because he remains with you
and will be within you.
I will not leave you orphaned;
I will come back to you.
A little while now and the world will see me no more;
but you see me
as one who has life, and you will have life.
On that day you will know
that I am in my Father,
and you in me, and I in you.
He who obeys the commandments he has from me
is the man who loves me;
and he who loves me will be loved by my Father.
I too will love him
and reveal myself to him."

In John's gospel, the reader comes across a word found in none of the other gospels: Paraclete. The Paraclete is the Holy Spirit, but the meaning of Paraclete may be clarified by such words as helper, counselor, comforter, or advocate. One might also apply these terms to Jesus, who demonstrated all these roles in his public ministry.

Jesus promised to send the Holy Spirit to help his followers after he was no longer with them. The Spirit is the presence of God in the lives of the disciples after the resurrection. Christians believe that this promised Holy Spirit came to and strengthened the group of believers on Pentecost Sunday. A Christian is called to trust in this unseen Spirit that resides within the believer. The root of this trust is the love between Jesus and the believer.

In an age as technologically oriented as ours, such talk of spiritual realities may indeed appear odd, and perhaps even a contradiction. Spiritual matters do not lend themselves to computer-like analysis, and so one may be inclined to avoid or dismiss them. Discussion of how one relates to Jesus Christ may be for some people an impossibility since, they assert, Jesus lived two thousand years ago. Yet to many Christians, such a discussion is full of possibilities that focus on the reality of new life born of the death and resurrection of Jesus and nourished by the Spirit of God.

Select a verse from the gospel reading. For this verse, ask yourself:

- What meaning does the verse have for me? Why?

____

____

____

____

Another theme from this reading is that of the love of Jesus for his disciples. Within John's gospel, this talk by Jesus appears soon after he had washed the feet of his disciples at the passover meal. This washing was a gesture of love, and came just before Jesus told his followers: "I give you a new commandment: love one another. As I have loved you, so you also should love one another. This is how all will know that you are my disciples, if you have love for one another" (13:34–35).

Jesus asks his followers to obey the commands he gives them as a sign of their love for him. Christians are challenged to keep the commandments first given to Moses centuries before Jesus was born. Indeed, Jesus had told his followers that he had come to fulfill the law and not to abolish it. The new commandment of Jesus does not replace the commandments given to Moses. Rather, it is an important moral foundation for living, for keeping the commandments, and for loving as Jesus loved.

Jesus' call to love is not just a plea to those who were present with him at that passover. It is a call to all people of good will, urging them not simply to love one another, but to love as Jesus had first loved them. This is a "spirit-love," a love whose source is God and whose expression is human love.

This description of love may become reality for some people, but for many love is an ideal, and at best no more than a glimpse of some future happiness. This may be just as true for a baptized person as it is for those who are catechumens. The catechumen, however, if part of a parish community rooted in the gospel, may be supported by others who are, in a living way, "Christ" to him or her. Such an awareness, though, unfortunately escapes many Christians.

Movement toward love is sometimes met by resistance and distrust. For some, unless an issue is in the newspapers, it does not exist at all. The evening news—with occasional spot reports on unsettling world conditions or conflict, mushrooming epidemics, latent racist attitudes, violence of various kinds, and so on—provides only a momentary glimpse of a lack of love that may not even affect the viewer or reader. These social issues remain hidden from many people's consciousness, while other love-denying realities occur on a more personal level: families whose members are not on speaking terms, neighborhoods where peace warrants exist between homeowners, employer-employee relations saddled by distrust and malice. Obviously, people's response to Jesus' call to them to love, to build the reign of God, has far to go. Yet Christians believe that they *can* indeed live as Jesus' disciples, and together accept his call and act on his mission. One question worth considering by a Christian, like you, may be, What can you do to chip away at anti-love values and attitudes of which you are aware?

To help you sort out what you might do to share in building a spirit of love in your family, community, or some other group, complete one or more of the following statements.

- To settle a conflict between ________________ and ________________

  I might ____

  ____

- To help me not judge others so hastily I might ________________

  ____

  ____

- To respond to a friend who has asked for my help in a personal matter that's just ripping him or her apart I might want to ________________

  ____

  ____

- To try to understand better an issue that I know about only from the media, I will

  ____

  ____

Now complete the Holy Spirit word-association that you started on page 186. List in the following chart the first four words that describe the Holy Spirit for you now that you have read the three scripture passages in this section.

Holy Spirit Word List "B"

After Reading Passages

1. ____________________ 3. ____________________

2. ____________________ 4. ____________________

- Do any of your choices surprise you? Why?

____

____

____

____

RENEWING YOUR LIFE OF FAITH

On page 192, four words were mentioned to describe God the Holy Spirit, the Paraclete: helper, counselor, comforter, and advocate. Are any of these words helpful in clarifying who the Spirit is for your life? Are one or more of the words you entered on page 196 more meaningful for you? You may need to uncover how what the words symbolize affects your attitudes and the way you try to live each day despite the obvious meanings of the words. The movement of the Spirit in your life cannot be assessed by some spiritual measuring rod. This would be a violation of what was stated in chapter 1 about developing as a whole person, and not as one who can be divided neatly into compartments such as emotional and physical.

One help for exploring the role of the Spirit in your life may be to recover, as Paul the apostle did, the Old Testament notion of the life-giving Spirit. Paul's New Testament writings have a variety of references to the Spirit as the life-giving and life-sustaining force in the world. For example, Paul points out that "Such confidence we have through Christ toward God.... [God] has indeed qualified us as ministers of a new covenant, not of letter but of spirit; for the letter brings death, but the Spirit gives life" (2 Corinthians 3:4–6).

Viewing the Spirit as life-giving and as the source of life may help you focus more clearly on the life that is yours as a newly baptized person. It may also lead you to explore how you are a source of life to others.

Recall your confirmation in the Spirit soon after your baptism. The celebration of the gift of the Spirit in your life affirmed and completed your baptism. In a sense, it provided you with the opportunity to confirm and be confirmed in your belief in the life-giving Spirit of God and of your decision to live "in the realm of the spirit."

Soon after experiencing the pouring of the baptismal water, you may have heard the celebrant pray during the laying on of hands:

> All-powerful God, Father of our Lord Jesus Christ,
> by water and the Holy Spirit
> you freed your sons and daughters from sin
> and gave them new life.
>
> Send your Holy Spirit upon them
> to be their helper and guide.

Give them the spirit of wisdom and understanding,
the spirit of right judgment and courage,
the spirit of knowledge and reverence.
Fill them with the spirit of wonder and awe in
your presence.

We ask this through Christ our Lord (*RCIA*, #234).[6]

While your godparent(s) stayed near you—with one or both placing the right hand on your shoulder—the celebrant anointed your forehead with chrism, saying, "N., be sealed with the Gift of the Holy Spirit" (*RCIA*, #235),[7] and making the sign of the cross as he did so. Like baptism, confirmation may never be repeated; the gift of the Holy Spirit is both life-giving and a gift for life, in union with the risen Christ.

For Cyril of Jerusalem, the newly anointed became partakers and followers of Christ. Speaking to the newly baptized in the fourth century, Cyril said:

Christ was anointed with a mystical oil of gladness; that is, with the Holy Spirit, called "oil of gladness" because He is the cause of spiritual gladness; so you, being anointed with ointment, have become partakers and fellows of Christ.[8]

- Cyril speaks of becoming followers of Christ; the prayer above mentions being given a variety of "spirits" to help the follower. Select one of these spirits, or gifts, and explore how it might apply to your life.

___

___

___

___

Food for People Who Are Moved by the Spirit: Eucharist

The powerful activity of the Spirit moves through and beyond baptism and confirmation. It is especially expressed in the eucharist and in the community of believers. The Spirit moves Christians to come together for worship and to go from worship to serve others.

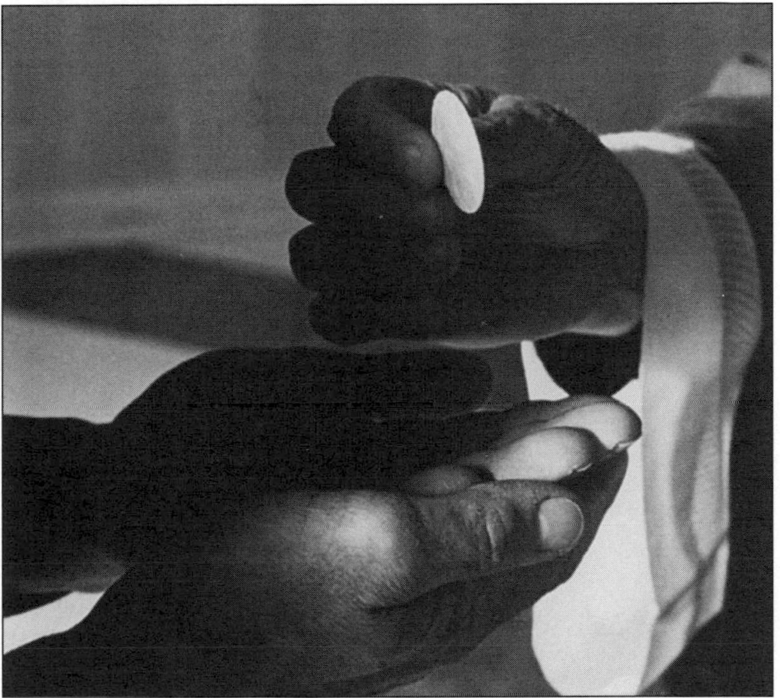

The Spirit of God calls a believer to be open to others in a spirit of compassion and trust. For a Christian, the nourishment needed to do this can be found when the community gathers together for the celebration of the eucharist. It is in this sacrament that the Spirit strengthens the believing community, the Church, for the days that follow.

For a baptized person, the call to serve others in Christ's name flows from entering into the mystery of Jesus' sacrificial meal and the sharing of eucharist by Christ's followers. From the weekly celebration of sharing the eucharist may arise the awareness of sharing one's life with others. The eucharist, celebrated regularly, is food for the journey of life, nourishing the believer and urging him or her to reach out to others.

- What might your sharing in the eucharist have to do with how you might try to serve others?

____

____

____

____

The eucharist, then, is not only an event that Christians gather for on a weekly basis. In the eucharist we praise and thank the Father of all. We express our common faith as a people gathered together in Christ. Indeed, the eucharist is a sacrament through which the Spirit transforms the worshipers into a Church with a mission which originates with Christ. There is an active quality to the sacrament that is beyond people's own doing. It is a sacrament that celebrates and calls forth the Spirit of God in the lives of those gathered together. For a Christian, like you, faith in Christ truly risen and really present in the eucharist may become a helpful influence in the way you choose to live. Of course, these are matters of faith, for without faith one may see no more than bread in the bread of life, and no more than wine in the cup of salvation and freedom. These words of Cyril of Jerusalem to newly baptized persons centuries ago may prove helpful to present-day Christians as well:

> Do not then think of the elements as bare bread and wine; they are, according to the Lord's declaration, the Body and Blood of Christ. Though sense suggests the contrary, let faith be your stay. Instead of judging the matter by taste, let faith give you an unwavering confidence that you have been privileged to receive the Body and Blood of Christ.[9]

Recall now not only your first celebration of eucharist at the time of your baptism, but also your present sharing in this sacrament. In chapter 5, the liturgy was discussed up to and including the beginning of the eucharistic prayer. As the presider continues the prayer on behalf of all present, he may say:

> Let your Spirit come upon these gifts to make them
> holy,
> so that they may become for us
> the body ✠ and blood of our Lord, Jesus Christ.[10]

The Spirit of God is called upon to make holy the simple gifts of bread and wine which are to become the body and blood of Christ. As the worshiping assembly continues its prayer, the priest says the words of Jesus over the bread and wine:

> Take this, all of you, and eat it:
> this is my body which will be given up for you. . . .
>
> Take this, all of you, and drink from it:
> this is the cup of my blood,
> the blood of the new and everlasting covenant.
> It will be shed for you and for all
> so that sins may be forgiven.
> Do this in memory of me.[11]

The assembly then proclaims and asserts with the presider the great truth of Christian faith:

> Christ has died,
> Christ is risen,
> Christ will come again.[12]

This mystery of faith is not to be understood fully but somehow glimpsed with eyes of faith. Our offering to the Father is made in memory of Jesus' death and resurrection. Our memorial is more than a simple act of remembering, however. In the mass we enter into Christ's saving death and resurrection. The sacrifice that Jesus offered on the cross is made real and present. We participate in this memorial today.

In exploring how a Christian may choose to respond to the gift of Jesus in the eucharist, one might take a clue from Ambrose of Milan. As you read this excerpt from one of Ambrose's Easter sermons to newly baptized Christians, try to identify how you have tried to help someone you know feel new again—for example, valued, worthwhile, or loved.

After the consecration I say to you that now there is the body of Christ. He Himself spoke and it was made; He Himself commanded and it was created. You yourself were, but you were an old creature; after you were consecrated, you began to be a new creature. Do you wish to know how a new creature? It says: "Every creature is new in Christ."[13]

- Ask yourself: What might I do this coming week that may show support for someone who is hurting? That may show I am "new in Christ"?

____

____

____

____

As the liturgy of the eucharist continues, the priest prays that all assembled will become more closely united by the Holy Spirit:

> May all of us who share in the body and blood of
> Christ
> be brought together in unity by the Holy Spirit.[14]

Christians' newness in Christ—or *re*newal—and union in the Spirit also emerge in the prayer of praise:

> Through him,
> with him,
> in him,
> in the unity of the Holy Spirit,
> all glory and honor is yours,
> almighty Father,
> for ever and ever. Amen.[15]

The liturgy continues with the communion rite, during which time each of the baptized is able to take and receive the body and blood of Christ. In the comm-*union*, believers are made one with Christ and the whole Church.

The preparation for communion includes, in part, the assembly's praying of the Our Father and sign of peace to one another. During your preparation for baptism, you may have been formally presented with the Our Father. The Our Father represents the prayer of the Church, and is itself the prayer Jesus taught to his followers when they asked him how to pray. You may want to pray this prayer now, perhaps as you first may have done as a catechumen.

> Our Father, who art in heaven
> hallowed be thy name;
> thy kingdom come;
> thy will be done on earth
> as it is in heaven.
> Give us this day our daily bread;
> and forgive us our trespasses
> as we forgive those
> who trespass against us;
> and lead us not into temptation,
> but deliver us from evil. Amen.

- What are your memories of the time when the Our Father was presented to you? What does this prayer mean to you now?

____

____

____

____

The sign of peace, discussed in the fifth chapter, and described by Cyril of Jerusalem as a sacred kiss, is not simply a handshake, but another sign of the unity in the Spirit among all who are assembled for worship. The assembly prays as one for the mercy and peace of the Lamb of God, and is able to approach the altar to share in the eucharist, the body of Christ—now broken before all to be shared with the community, together as one in Christ. In the fifth century, Augustine would tell Christians:

> If, therefore, you are the Body of Christ and His members, your mystery is presented at the table of the Lord: you receive your mystery. To that which you are, you answer: "Amen"; and by answering, you subscribe to it. For you hear: "The Body of Christ!" and you answer: "Amen!" Be a member of Christ's Body, so that your "Amen" may be the truth.[16]

Cyril of Jerusalem urged the newly baptized to approach the eucharist this way, saying:

> Making your left hand a throne for the right (for it is about to receive a King) and cupping your palm, so receive the Body of Christ; and answer: "Amen." . . . Give thanks to the God who has deigned to admit you to such high mysteries.[17]

The quotations from Cyril (page 200), Ambrose (page 202), and Augustine (page 204) all seem to emphasize the divinity of Christ. This is not surprising, since all these preachers lived during a time when Christ's divine nature was being challenged. The church at the time countered by strongly asserting that Christ was indeed divine.

Jesus, truly human and truly divine, is really present in the eucharist under the appearances of bread and wine. Each time you join with your parish for the celebration of eucharist, you are invited to renew your life of faith and reassert what it means for you to be a Christian. Part of this reassertion is in seeing Christ with you and your parish, for example, in the scriptures, in the assembly gathered together for worship, and in the presider. The baptized are called, by the way they live, to become the body of Christ in the unity of the Holy Spirit. Indeed, you continue to become as your journey continues and as you share the Bread of life broken and given for all, as one body in Christ.

Reflect now on the Spirit who motivates you to worship and to adhere to the faith you professed at your baptism. For a Christian, like you, the Spirit of God may not only beckon one to gather with others for eucharist, but also may move one to act in Jesus' name. In the words of Theodore of Mopsuestia to the newly baptized:

> And the priest prays that the grace of the Holy Spirit may come also on all those present, in order that as they have been perfected into one body in the likeness of the second birth, so also they may be knit here as if into one body by the communion of the flesh of our Lord, and in order also that they may embrace and follow one purpose with concord, peace, and diligence in good works.[18]

- Concord: This is another word for harmony. Can you identify one situation for which you can be a source of harmony?

____

____

____

____

- Peace: Are you experiencing a need for peace in your life now? What is it and what might you do about it?

____

____

____

____

- Good Works: Is one's faith in God sufficient for the Christian? Or is such faith a starting point? The Catholic Church teaches that faith and good works are essential. The gospel passage on page 192 also points out the need for keeping the commandments "he has from me" [Christ]. What do you think? Are faith *and* good works essential for you? Is there a challenge for you here?

____

____

____

____

Did You Know?

Near the end of the Easter season is the feast of the ascension. On this day Christians recall Jesus' return to the Father following his resurrection. Three scripture readings are proclaimed:

- The first is from the beginning of the Acts of the Apostles (1:1–11). This passage includes the scriptural account of Jesus' ascension: "He was lifted up before their eyes in a cloud which took him from their sight."
- The second reading is from Paul's letter to the Ephesians (1:17–23). Paul calls the God of Jesus "the Father of glory" and asserts his belief in Christ as "head of the church, which is his body: the fullness of him who fills the universe in all its parts."
- The last reading is from the final verses of the gospel according to Matthew (28:16–20). In this gospel ending, the risen Jesus commissions the eleven disciples to go and baptize others "in the name of the Father, and of the Son, and of the Holy Spirit." Jesus assures his followers that he will be with them always. Each of these readings describes an aspect of Christian teaching. During the next week, select one of these readings for your own reflection. For the reading you select, try to determine how it might apply to your life. For example, the belief that Jesus is always present is accepted by many Christians. But what does it mean for you? How is Jesus present in the circumstances of your life?

You may want to use the space below to jot down some thoughts during the week to help you explore these questions.

ACCEPTING THE CHALLENGE

One of the statements of the fathers of the church appearing earlier in this chapter (page 183) was this one: "For whatever the Holy Spirit touches is hallowed and changed." For a believing Christian, the Spirit of God may indeed be a source for change, for self-discovery, and for decision-making. A baptized person may not look any different following reception of the sacraments. However, that person may undergo an inner change rooted in his or her faith in Jesus Christ. Somehow, all that influenced Jesus, all that he made his own, becomes available to others. The Spirit of God touches baptized people and enables believers to live as followers of Christ.

What is the relation between the Spirit and the eucharist? Four aspects of the eucharist may help a Christian, like you, to link the Spirit with the eucharist, and then go beyond that to link your faith with the way you live it. The four aspects, rooted in the Church's celebration of the liturgy, are:

- eucharist as meal;
- eucharist as thanksgiving;
- eucharist as real presence of Christ;
- eucharist as sacrifice.

Four actions identified with eucharist as meal are taking, blessing, breaking, and sharing. A Christian takes the sacred bread in preparation for the meal; it is blessed as an offering of all present during the eucharistic prayer; it is broken and shared among the congregation during the communion. What situations from your life remind you of one of these actions? Tell about it here. When might you:

- take: ______________________________

- bless: ______________________________

- break: ______________________________

- share: ______________________________

The root meaning of the word eucharist is thanksgiving. Christians offer in thanks to God the One who gave himself for us. What impact can thanksgiving have on your life? What are you thankful for? The Spirit moves a Christian, like you, to thank God for the gift of Jesus in the eucharist. Indeed, the whole eucharistic prayer is an expression of thanksgiving to God. How else do you offer thanks in your life?

The real presence of Christ has been, perhaps, one of the most difficult aspects of faith for people to believe in. How, after all, can the bread and wine be Jesus? Catholic belief asserts that the bread and wine really become the body and blood of Christ. What appears to be bread and wine is no longer bread and wine, but Christ himself.

Sharing in the eucharist is not just for those who do so, but also has as its goal the unity of the Church brought about by the Holy Spirit. For a Christian, another question may be how one is actually present to and united with others. You may want to ask yourself: How can I be happy and at peace with others? How will I be a sign of Christ's presence to others?

Finally, the eucharist is a sacrifice. It is a sacrifice of Christ and of all assembled, an offering of Christ and our whole selves to the Father. We enter into this sacred memorial. The faithful look to God for the strength to serve others in the name of Jesus. The Spirit calls newly baptized persons to participate in the sacrifice and to commit themselves to living as best they can in the Spirit of Christ.

Looking Back

As you look back on this chapter, think about the two words used most frequently here: Spirit and eucharist. Decide if you really are willing to allow God the Holy Spirit to work with you in your daily life. Then respond to each of these sections for reviewing the scriptures of the sixth Sunday of Easter (pages 184-196).

- Acts of the Apostles 8:5–8, 14–17—Who or what might cause me to rejoice? Not to be just happy, but really be joyful?

  ____

  ____

  ____

  ____

- 1 Peter 3:15–18—A person who, for me, is a symbol of the hope that Christians believe in is ______________________________

  This is because . . .

  ____

  ____

  ____

  ____

- John 14:15–21—In this reading Jesus says, "you will have life." What does this life Jesus is speaking about mean to me? (One or more of the following phrases may help you to explore this thought.)

- Life is waking up each day knowing that ____________________

  ____

- Life is feeling in my heart that ____________________

  ____

- Life really means love because ________________________________

____

- Life is really memories that remain alive because ________________

____

For the section of the chapter on renewing your life of faith (pages 196-207), ask yourself: Is the Spirit . . .

_____ hard to understand?
_____ present in some way but not in a way I can describe?
_____ moving me to act in a certain way?
_____ new life for me?
_____ moving me to act differently at home or at work?

Focus, too, on the presence of the Spirit in the celebration of the eucharist. Somehow, mysteriously, the Spirit unites the believers; perhaps some of the worshipers will themselves be transformed. Ask yourself:

- How will I draw more closely to:

_____ a close friend _____ a child

_____ a spouse _____ a parent

____

____

____

____

- What will I have to discover in myself to strengthen the way I relate to another person?

____

____

____

____

As you explore what it is that brings you together with others in the eucharist, you may discover more about yourself in light of the Spirit, worship, or others. Perhaps this journey within yourself is the most important fruit of all you did to prepare for eucharist and all you may do as a baptized person. These words of Cyril of Jerusalem may be especially appropriate for you:

"May the God of peace sanctify you completely, and may your whole spirit, soul and body be preserved blameless at the coming of our Lord Jesus Christ," [1 Thess. 5:23] whose is the glory now and evermore, world without end. Amen.[19]

7

Your Mission for Your Life of Faith

PSALM–PRAYER

The LORD is my light and my salvation;
whom do I fear?
The LORD is my life's refuge;
of whom am I afraid?…

One thing I ask of the LORD;
this I seek:
To dwell in the LORD'S house
all the days of my life,
To gaze on the LORD's beauty,
to visit his temple.…

Hear my voice, LORD, when I call;
have mercy on me and answer me.
"Come," says my heart, "seek God's face";
your face, LORD, do I seek!

Psalm 27: 1, 4, 7–8

Overview

The television show "Mission: Impossible" began with a challenge and a choice for the curious listener: to carry out a daring and seemingly impossible mission. Now, as you begin this last chapter, it is hoped that you can say, "Mission: Possible." This chapter is intended to encourage you to explore the mission you see for yourself as a Christian. It remains your choice to accept as your own Christ's mission to his followers. The chapter may aid in uncovering what this mission could mean for your life as you continue to grow with your parish community.

The chapter also links the notion of mission for a life of faith to the eucharist. The celebration of the eucharist has been treated in these final three chapters because the nourishment of the eucharist is so vital to the life of the baptized. The eucharist is nourishment, really, for living as a Christian in whatever way you choose.

As with the other chapters, there are spaces for you to record your thoughts as you read. You may also wish to discuss some of your reflections or decisions with a family member, godparent, or friend.

EXPLORING YOUR EXPERIENCE

Being reborn of water and the Spirit is not an ending, but a continuation of what has already been begun—your mission for your life of faith. It would seem odd to contend that your faith is some object you have now that you are baptized. Conversion to a Christian way of life usually takes time. That is why the word journey has been used in this book. Journeys take time. Often, they take commitment, risk, challenge, change, and pain. The journey for a newly baptized person, like you, hopefully will continue beyond this last chapter.

Your journey as a Christian is one that is not duplicated exactly by others. With your own beliefs, values, and attitudes, you may feel that you are discovering anew what it is to live in the Spirit of God in your daily life. No one can live your faith, believe, or carry out your mission for you. Your personal search for meaning in life that may have been capsulized during the catechumenate may continue for a lifetime. Baptism is not just the end of a spiritual journey, but a transition, or passage, inviting you to explore further what it is for you to be a Christian, a disciple of the risen Lord.

One's mission for a life shaped by the Spirit of Christ does not usually emerge as if it were a response to a computer command:

> GO TO INPUT A & SEE PANEL B FOR FURTHER INSTRUCTIONS. PROCEED TO TYPE. RESULT IS MISSION FOR YOUR LIFE = JOURNEY OVER. PROCEED AT ONCE TO INPUT B. WHEN CONVERSION PROGRAM OVER, MISSION IS COMPLETED.

One's mission for a life of faith can develop in many ways. Often it is an experience over time, and not some sudden awareness based on a single moment in time. Otherwise, the period after your baptism could become no more than a time of relief that the preparation, anticipation, and yearning are over. This is part of the mystery of baptism. In finding Jesus, who came to give life to the full, one can begin to seek him even more.

Sometimes it is helpful to look for examples of how others have chosen to live their commitment to Christian faith. Such examples are not suggestions for how all should live, but helps for exploring the sense of mission that would lead a person to live in a certain way. In other words, the person described is one example of conversion and journeying in faith, and not some prescribed model for all Christians. With this in mind, you may benefit from the following story. It tells of a woman whose mission for life included working with, learning from, and struggling for people in a country in South America. Read on to discover how one person chose to live out her baptism.

A Story of C.M.

C.M. moved from North America to a South American city, eager to begin her new work with the poor of the barrios. She had lived for many years in the United States, working as a teacher, school principal, and in other administrative positions. Prior to that had been a period of time in Borneo. For C.M., a Franciscan missionary, the latest move was an opportunity to assert in a new and challenging way her mission as a Christian and acceptance of the Christian message.

In a letter to friends during one Christmas season, C.M. wrote of a woman named Vicky. Vicky had four small children and was raising them on her own. The family lived on an allowance of three dollars a month per child and other small donations. C.M. noted in her letter that:

> Vicky...got word early in December that she had to move out of the field where she had been living as a construction company was coming in to start building. During the two weeks before Christmas we tramped the streets looking for someone who would rent her a piece of their yard to put up her "house." We eventually found something and the day before Christmas Eve got everything settled. She was asked by the community to play the part of Mary with her baby son as the Baby during Midnight Mass—for the dramatization of the gospel. It was indeed very appropriate. As she went from door to door as Mary all I could think of was how she and I had walked the streets just a week or so before. We had a good Christmas....Vicky had a house.[1]

C.M.'s concern for the poor was revealed in two subsequent letters. They also seemed to show a heightened awareness of the tenuous political situation where she was, plus a keen unwillingness to sacrifice her personal values. C.M. wrote the following in a letter describing events during a national strike:

> Ink on a page cannot transmit the fear, the pain, the anger, the brutality, the courage that touched us all one way or another, but most especially the poor. . . .
>
> We ourselves have, for one reason or another, faced machine guns, tear gas, etc. almost every second day lately. The toll it takes on the human person is incredible. Yet the capacity that we all have to continue for people and values we believe in!
>
> There are signs of hope though we are far from reaching our goal. I suppose the hope is continually there but it is in the constancy of all our actions that our hopes will be realized. We will continue in our discontent until there is justice. The challenge is not to become accustomed.[2]

C.M.'s sense of determination to carry on the mission she felt called to do was perhaps a large part of her own journey of faith. There appeared to be a hope alive in her that survived in the middle of oppressive living conditions. One may indeed wonder what kept C.M. going. A hint of her motivation, or perhaps even ongoing conversion, may be seen from some remarks about the bonds of friendship in a later letter:

> Our hopes are raised by the women with whom we share our lives and work. Our work with women continues to grow and so do we through the sharing and solidarity we experience. The bonds of friendship among all of us women are what give us support and hope. The isolation that is forced on us through poverty, silence and violence, we are consciously breaking down. We are looking at some of our internal repressive messages that have kept us apart and bound us to a system of power and dominance. . . .
>
> Together we [women] are learning to make the connections between the oppression and violence of the State and of the Home. . . .

> Women open their homes to other women giving them temporary shelter. We all open our hearts to one another giving encouragement and support. We begin to recognize the worth of the self and that of other women; to take one another seriously. We are creating a space for ourselves, a space that is called Friendship. In that space we are coming to recognize a Power that is greater than each of us or all of us.[3]

C.M.'s close identity with women suffering from state or home oppression seemed to have strengthened her in a very difficult and challenging situation. Her hope appeared to be made of a determination and a rugged spirit that refused to surrender to Goliath-like forces beckoning her to give up. She had chosen to immerse herself in what might have appeared to the outside observer as a no-win situation. Yet she was sustained by "a Power that is greater than each of us or all of us." One may suggest that her mission was molded by a deep sense of justice and a desire to affirm all people as people of God, with the right to a decent life.

- Do you know of someone of great hope and strength who is facing overwhelming odds? What do you think keeps this person going?

____

____

____

____

- When you hear a priest or other preacher say "You have a mission!" what do you think of first? Why is that?

____

____

____

____

Throughout this book you have been asked to show by how you live what your faith means to you. This is all part of coming to grips with your mission for a life of faith. As you continue your journey, how might you live your faith commitment?

____

____

____

____

C.M.'s mission may be rooted in a strong faith and awareness of God's presence in life. More obviously, it could be suggested that C.M.'s conversion to Christ can be seen in her service to others and in her attempts to help them be free from whatever enslaved them.

Not content to watch others suffer, C.M. seemed to have entered into the situation of others by promoting in her own life what those around her were seeking—peace, and a trust in God's presence with each new day. Her mission, in other words, was lived out in her daily life—not only an "I believe!" to statements of faith, but also a genuine attempt to put these beliefs into action. Her commitment also seems consistent with these words of a newly baptized person:

> As I was approaching baptism I felt that that would tie everything together for me...and then I would be this person that would stand up and...this is what I believe in and I'd have a foundation to believe in it.

One does not have to "stand up" in the same way as C.M. to be a committed Christian. For example, sometimes people in suburban settings wonder why their life setting is not as sparse as those in other areas of the world. Or a family may be comfortably settled in a pleasant city apartment, and somehow sense an injustice in their good fortune when compared to people they read about in other parts of the world.

Short of traveling to faraway places to provide direct assistance, the fortunate few can provide highly effective assistance to people in their local surroundings. Often these people's needs go undetected . . . and unmet. For example, some people do not know that "children are the poorest members of our society—one out of five children grows up poor in the richest nation on earth."[4] In line with this thinking, read this statement of a newly baptized woman regarding her work as a teacher. It reveals a stick-to-itiveness on her part that demonstrates an unwillingness to give in to pressure in a challenging situation. When asked if her lifestyle or way of looking at situations in her life had changed as a result of being a catechumen, she replied:

> Well, I look at things in a different light now...I teach emotionally disturbed children. Some weeks are better than others. This year I have a very large class. There's this one boy, who is no longer with me. There's days when they get me so aggravated...they're acting out and I know why they're acting out. But dealing with it on a daily basis, sometimes personal problems get intermingled with everything. I'll get really upset with them and then at recess my assistant takes them out and I'll

> take a deep breath and think about why this happened or whatever. I can always find something positive in it, and you know it's not their fault, and this is what they're trying to say.

- Think about your home, school, or job. When do you feel especially challenged? Why?

  ____

  ____

  ____

  ____

- What keeps you going when things get tough? How?

  ____

  ____

  ____

  ____

EXPLORING THE SCRIPTURES

A newly baptized person, in embracing a life of discipleship, is able to participate in Jesus' mission with other Christians. Mutual support among parish members and their joint celebration of the sacraments may strengthen one's willingness to assist others and to shape an attitude of faith conceived before becoming (or as) a catechumen and born in baptism.

One may especially feel the need for such support when facing difficult or challenging situations.

The experience of maintaining hope and moving ahead in the face of adversity is one that Jesus shared. Three times Jesus forecast his own death (Luke 9:21–27; 9:44–45; 18:31–34). He was criticized for forgiving sins and for healing on the sabbath. He was expelled from Nazareth and rebuked Peter for presuming he would not have to suffer and die, saying, "Get behind me, Satan! You are an obstacle to me. You are thinking not as God does, but as human beings do" (Matthew 16:23). Fully divine and fully human, Jesus experienced the ups and downs of life as did others of his time—in all things but sin.

One of the characteristics of Jesus' life was the consolation he found in prayer. The scripture readings for the seventh Sunday of Easter focus in part on the prayer of Jesus and the early disciples of the Church. Jesus frequently turned to God for prayer. He called God "Abba," the Aramaic word for father. Jesus' mission was indeed as he had said in the temple:

> "The Spirit of the Lord is upon me,
> because he has anointed me
> to bring glad tidings to the poor.
> He has sent me to proclaim liberty to captives
> and recovery of sight to the blind,
> to let the oppressed go free,
> and to proclaim a year acceptable to the Lord"
> (Luke 4:18-19).

Beneath this mission, and supporting it, was a strong connection to his Father in prayer. The letter to the Hebrews states that "In the days when he was in the flesh, he offered prayers and supplications with loud cries and tears to the one who was able to save him from death, and he was heard because of his reverence" (5:7).

For a Christian, like you, prayer and personal reflection may result in hearing pleas for assistance from human service and other care-giving organizations that may have no formal connection to parish life. Many Christians are active in supporting these outreach efforts. The motivation to serve may be rooted in Jesus' words quoted above and in the belief that Jesus called people to God.

As you read the scripture passages that follow, try to think about your mission as a Christian and your attitude toward continuing your journey of faith. Ask yourself:

- Why do you now believe as a Christian?

____

____

____

____

The Scriptures of the Seventh Sunday of Easter

The readings of the seventh Sunday of the Easter season are from the Acts of the Apostles, the first letter of Peter, and the gospel according to John.

Acts of the Apostles 1:12–14

The center of the early Church was Jerusalem. This historic and rebuilt city was no stranger to religious groups, and so the disciples elect to return and stay together there. As you read the passage, try to identify one or more important journeys of your own. Think about why you traveled and what you experienced when you arrived.

[After Jesus was taken up into the heavens,] the apostles returned to Jerusalem from the mount called Olivet near Jerusalem, a mere sabbath's journey away. Entering the city, they went to the upstairs room where they were staying: Peter and John and James and Andrew;

Philip and Thomas, Bartholomew and Matthew; James son of Alpheus; Simon, the Zealot party member, and Judas son of James. Together they devoted themselves to constant prayer. There were some women in their company and Mary the mother of Jesus, and his brothers.

This passage begins just after Jesus was taken from the sight of his disciples. The verse preceding the passage includes the message of two men dressed in white: "Men of Galilee,...why are you standing there looking at the sky? This Jesus who has been taken up from you into heaven will return in the same way as you have seen him going into heaven" (1:11). Perhaps out of anticipation of Jesus' return, the disciples return to Jerusalem. As the passage points out, they occupied themselves with prayer.

Prayer was an important part of the disciples' discernment of their mission in following in Jesus' footsteps. One may wonder what went through the disciples' minds as they prayed together. The mysterious happenings of the previous days may have left them awe-filled yet confused. And now Jesus bids them farewell and vanishes from their sight!

What may be helpful for a Christian today is the notion that when one thinks that Jesus is absent from one's life, that may just be the right time to turn to prayer. You may want to stop here and ask yourself:

- When do I pray? Why do I pray?

____

____

____

____

Some people may think of prayer as no more than asking God for "things to turn out OK." Prayer is much deeper than that. Through prayer one may pause and discover in the quiet of one's heart the presence of the Spirit of God. Such discovery may be a source of strength to rebuild an uncertain relationship, to move ahead to an unexpected future, or to maintain the status quo with renewed hope. Prayer can be an important help as you live your mission for your life of faith.

In addition to the "asking God" type of prayer, one may pray in a spirit of contrition, of praise, or of thanks. Prayer forms such as journal-keeping, centering prayer, or charismatic prayer may also help you to explore your mission as a Christian. Keeping a journal may help you explore issues that are important to your life. Centering prayer is just what its name implies—a method of clearing one's mind of thoughts and distractions and gently resting in the presence of the Spirit of God. Charismatic prayer is characterized by an intense personal experience of the Holy Spirit alone or with others. Indeed, each gathering for eucharist is an opportunity to pray with others in thanksgiving to God for the gift of Jesus really present in this sacrament—and to assert with other believers the willingness of the local parish to put into practice what it has professed in faith. In this way the parish may be able to clarify its own mission as a Christian community, a community of discipleship.

To help you to explore prayer in your life, complete one or more of the following statements.

- Prayer enables me to ______________________________

____

____

- When it comes to prayer I wish that I ____________________

____

____

- Someone who is an example of a prayerful person for me is ______________ ______________________. This is because ______________________________ ____

- A person's whole life can really be a prayer because ____________________ ____ ____

1 PETER 4:13–16

The theme for this reading is in a sense a return to a theme discussed earlier, that of suffering. In Chapter 4, the second reading from 1 Peter 2:20–25 also dealt with suffering. As with other reflections on this topic, think briefly of two or three recent events that may remind you of people's struggles in life. Ask yourself if any good could possibly result from the suffering or struggles.

Rejoice, insofar as you share Christ's sufferings. When his glory is revealed you will rejoice exultantly. Happy are you when you are insulted for the sake of Christ, for then God's Spirit in its glory has come to rest on you. See to it that none of you suffers for being a murderer, a thief, a malefactor, or a destroyer of another's rights. If anyone suffers for being a Christian, however, he ought not be ashamed. He should rather glorify God in virtue of that name.

As noted in chapter 2, Peter addresses his comments to Christians who are gentiles in Asia Minor. He urges them to maintain their identity as Christians in the face of unkindness from their neighbors who are not part of their religious body.

Rejoicing in one's suffering is a belief that is unusual and peculiar, yet characteristically Christian. Why would anyone be happy over one's own suffering? Or over physical torment? The reason Peter gives for being happy over suffering is that a Christian bears such suffering for the name of Christ, and the ultimate effect of such suffering will be life forever with the risen Christ.

The reading points out that God's Spirit is with those who suffer. For a baptized person, Jesus' suffering and death on the cross is a particularly sacred yet challenging dimension of what it means to live as a Christian. Ongoing spiritual direction may help a Christian to discover levels of meaning of this and other aspects of Christian belief. It may also help one to discern the promptings of the Spirit in one's life.

Today, it is not uncommon to hear that suffering must be eliminated. One can name numerous cases of people suffering: travel accidents, family violence, disease, emotional and physical abuse, and so on. However, there are other types of suffering that people experience. These are certain sufferings of the heart, characterized by a willingness to accept the consequences of a decision, however difficult, for what one believes must be done. In fact, the decision may be one over which the person or group has no control; the situation may involve physical torment as well. For example, the great tragedy of the Holocaust includes stories of heroism and risk on the part of a people determined to survive despite incredible odds against them.

Obviously, people suffer for various reasons. Indeed, the intensity of people's beliefs may prevent them from accepting what may appear to be too much of a compromise.

Look at the following list of some types of suffering people may endure:

Types of Suffering

physical	social
emotional	religious
intellectual	mental

Is there someone you know who is experiencing one or more of these kinds of suffering? What could you do to express your care for that person? Will you do it?

____

____

____

____

Look again at the list. Is there a type of suffering listed that you are enduring? If so, how might your faith in Christ help you to deal with it?

____

____

____

____

JOHN 17:1–11

The gospel reading is Jesus' great prayer before he was arrested and sentenced to death. His prayer reveals a unique intimacy with God, whom he calls Father. As you read the passage, you may want to think about your own experience of prayer, its impact on your life of faith, and on how you relate to God.

Jesus looked up to heaven and said:
"Father, the hour has come!
Give glory to your Son
that your Son may give glory to you,

inasmuch as you have given him authority over all mankind,
that he may bestow eternal life on those you gave him.
(Eternal life is this:
to know you, the only true God,
and him whom you have sent, Jesus Christ.)
I have given you glory on earth
by finishing the work you gave me to do.
Do you now, Father, give me glory at your side,
a glory I had with you before the world began.
I have made your name known
to those you gave me out of the world.
These men you gave me were yours;
they have kept your word.
Now they realize
that all that you gave me comes from you.
I entrusted to them
the message you entrusted to me,
and they received it.
They have known that in truth I came from you,
they have believed it was you who sent me.

"For these I pray—
not for the world
but for these you have given me,
for they are really yours.
(Just as all that belongs to you is yours,
so all that belongs to you is mine.)
It is in them that I have been glorified.
I am in the world no more,
but these are in the world
as I come to you."

The prayer that Jesus utters is delivered with intensity. He is about to undergo arrest, suffering, and death. He turns to his Father in prayer and in so doing recalls his mission on earth: "I have given you glory on earth by finishing the work you gave me to do." Jesus also reflects on the faithfulness of his disciples, noting their acceptance of his own ministry and message.

Throughout this book Jesus' work has been identified with the word mission. The opening part of the section on the scriptures (pages 221-223) refers to Jesus' mission. But Jesus' work was not limited to doing helpful things for people; in healing and comforting others, Jesus, Christians believe, was revealing God to them. In doing this, he helped people begin to discover and even taste the life of God that is described by the word eternal. When Jesus prayed, "I have made your name known," he may have been telling God more than "Now they know what to call you." Jesus may have really been acknowledging who he was and is in revealing and sharing with others the very life of God.

- Imagine yourself alongside the first followers of Jesus. You hear him say the words of this passage. Is there a part of the passage that puzzles you? What is it? What would you ask Jesus to help you understand better?

____

____

____

____

- Do you consider knowing God to be the same as knowing about God? Which, for you, is the more challenging way to view God? Why is that?

____

____

____

____

Christians may view their mission as one of carrying on the work of Jesus in the course of their daily life experiences.

With this in mind, complete the following:

- An everyday experience of mine that might enable me to live what I believe as a Christian is ______________________________

  ____

  ____

  This is because ______________________________

  ____

In his prayer Jesus expresses confidence in his followers. He is obviously pleased with their acceptance of his mission and his love for them. He really believed in them. He also felt deeply for his disciples.

How do you show you believe not only in God but also in others? This question is somewhat of an echo of the one in chapter 1 in which you were asked to identify what it meant to say you believed in yourself, God, Jesus, and the Church. Now, as you near the end of this book, reflect on why you believe in others. Use the following chart to help you get started.

Belief in Others

People I Believe in	*Why I Believe in Them*	*One Word to Describe Each Person*
1.		
2.		
3.		

Now reread slowly Jesus' prayer on pages 228-229. Perhaps you can make his prayer your own as you discover the joy of being newly baptized and of exploring your mission for a life of faith. Indeed, the opening words of Jesus may summarize some of your thoughts from the night of your baptism: "Father, the hour has come!"

RENEWING YOUR LIFE OF FAITH

In all the previous chapters you have been encouraged to renew the life of faith that began long before your baptism. However, you may have wondered why there was a need for such a renewal; after all, you are newly baptized, so why the need to renew your baptism now?

For a Christian, the time after baptism is no less important than the time before. But like the time before, it is very important to experience the sustaining nourishment of supportive people. This is experienced preeminently in the weekly gathering for eucharist—an opportunity to make new again, to renew, with the parish assembly what you professed at your baptism. It is also an opportunity to reflect on your life resulting from the eucharistic celebration—your mission for your life of faith as a disciple of the risen One.

Consider now the concluding parts of the eucharistic liturgy and what they may mean for your life. During this brief conclusion to the mass the priest or deacon encourages all present to serve others in the name of God. The priest prays, "The Lord be with you," and all assembled respond, "And also with you." The priest blesses the congregation, and he or the deacon urges all to "go in peace to love and serve the Lord."[5] The call to service is a reminder of Jesus' plea to his disciples to "love one another. As I have loved you, so you also should love one another" (John 13:34). For a Christian, like you, it may be a call to live this mission by making sense of how your sharing in the eucharist may affect your daily experiences with others.

In chapter 6 four ways of understanding eucharist were presented: as meal, thanksgiving, real presence of Christ, and sacrifice. The way you choose to live out the faith you express when you gather with your parish for mass may be described by one or more of these meanings—and by other meanings, also. For example, if you think just for a moment of the meal aspect, you may want to consider your own meal-taking and how you may or may not take your eating habits for granted. This may lead to thoughts about the diet urge in this country and the lack of food in other nations and in pockets of the United States as well.

In treating eucharist as thanksgiving, you may want to reflect on your attitude of thanks in other aspects of your life. For example, one may be grateful for receiving a negative medical report or for discovering a long lost friend.

The real presence of Christ may lead to reflection on how the grace of holy communion may move believers toward a spirit of unity as the Church. It may also lead to seeing Christ in others or trying to bring the presence of Christ to others. You may want to ask yourself how you try to see goodness in a person who is difficult to live or work with or how you try to enable others to bring out the best in themselves.

Finally, you may decide at some point to explore what eucharist as sacrifice may mean for you.

The ultimate sacrifice is Jesus' complete and total giving of himself for all humanity. Through his passion, death, and resurrection—the paschal mystery—Jesus gains and sustains for us life with God, not for one day, one year, or one decade, but forever.

A commonly understood meaning for sacrifice is giving up something for another. However, there are other meanings worth considering. For example, fasting has traditionally been one means of sacrifice for many Christians. The prophet Isaiah provides what may be a more challenging meaning for some people. He says:

> This, rather, is the fasting that I wish:
> releasing those bound unjustly,
> untying the thongs of the yoke;
> Setting free the oppressed,
> breaking every yoke;

Sharing your bread with the hungry,
    sheltering the oppressed and the homeless;
Clothing the naked when you see them,
    and not turning your back on your own.
        (Isaiah 58:6–7)

Isaiah goes on to speak of God's blessing in all who live as the prophet has described. Perhaps this understanding of fasting will open up new ways for you to reexamine the meaning of sacrifice for your life. Sacrifice may then be seen as saying yes to the presence of the risen Christ in one's life.

At the end of mass, when the priest or deacon urges all to go in peace, you may want to think of one or more of these meanings of eucharist as a possible way to live what you believe your mission is as a baptized person. One fourth-century preacher, Theodore of Mopsuestia, had this to say about the concluding part of the eucharistic celebration. Note his emphasis on thanksgiving:

After you have received the communion you rightly and spontaneously offer thanksgiving and praise to God, so that you may not be ungrateful with regard to this Divine gift. And you remain (in the Church), so that you may also offer thanksgiving and praise with every one, according to the regulations of the Church, because it behoves [sic] all those who received this spiritual food to offer thanksgiving to God publicly for this great gift.[6]

Theodore, however, urges on his newly baptized listeners to link thanksgiving for spiritual gifts to living according to the moral principles of their faith. He tells them:

We ought . . . to endeavour to make ourselves worthy, as much as possible, of the Sacrament; and we shall be worthy of it if we obey the commandments of Christ our Lord, who promised afore these and similar benefits to us, if we strive to turn away from evil things and cleave to good things, and to reject cruelty and adopt mercy, which brought us benefits such as these. . . . We will all the more not receive the grace and the benefits prepared for us by God, while still in this world, if we do not strive with all our power to have mercy upon our neighbours.[7]

Theodore links receiving the eucharist to living as a Christian. For him, one flows from the other. Imagine you are in Theodore's congregation. Would you have any questions for him? If so, what would they be?

- How would you explain to another baptized person the relation between worshiping at mass and living as a Christian?

A Look at Ministry

The mission for a life of faith for a Christian is not only to gather with others for the eucharistic celebration, or to avoid questionable behavior forbidden by the Ten Commandments. A Christian is called to carry out one's mission and live out the faith believed and celebrated in eucharist in an outreach to others that is called ministry.

One's ministry to others may provide a newly baptized person with a sense of looking more closely at one's journey of faith. As noted elsewhere, the journey of faith is not ended at baptism, but really only begins in a new and perhaps mysterious way. This does not mean that life for a Christian is some sort of rainbow existence characterized by peak moments of wonder, awe, and joy. Conversion to Christ may be for a Christian, like you, an ongoing journey that includes doubt as well as faith, a sense of loss as well as hope, sadness as well as joy. It may also include a vibrant prayer life which is nourished by the sacraments of the Church.

The newly baptized person quoted below found that, despite her good intentions, time flew by and she was unable to participate after baptism as she had before. She said:

> That first year I didn't go at all [to the catechumenate meetings]....In a way it was a letdown, that first year being married and I just started working. Before I knew it, the whole year was over. I didn't even remember the year. Last year I remember coming to a few meetings, because I really wanted that back. I really wanted to see everybody again, and I think I came to like three meetings and then it was open school night, and it was this...then I couldn't go for like four weeks. Then I felt like I wasn't finishing something I was starting, and I just didn't go. And this summer, I think maybe in July or so, there was something in the [parish] bulletin...to myself I was really thinking about it, "I would really like to go back, wouldn't it be great if I could sponsor somebody and really become involved in it."
>
> I was trying to think of people I knew, and I thought of this one friend....It was like the Lord knew what I wanted....I guess she [my friend] did know that I always wasn't a Catholic and this was a new thing to me. And I just tried to give her a brief rundown of the program, which is really hard to do. And then I had said to her, "Well, there's a meeting on such and such a day," and she said, "I'll check it out." And she went,...and she thought the people were great....And you know, I'm really glad that I came back.

Perhaps this person is being too hard on herself: with a new marriage and a new job, she had plenty to take care of as far as a mission for her life was concerned. Yet she still felt the need to continue her involvement in introducing others to the Church. In talking with her friend, she apparently felt a sense of participation in the parish's catechumenate ministry.

- There are many ways to help in parish ministry. Parish life may include ministries in such diverse areas as catechesis, worship, Christian initiation sponsor, justice and peace work, social services, physical plant upkeep, communications, and so on. Now that you are baptized, have you begun to explore ways of staying active in your parish? If so, how?

____

____

____

____

- How do you view participation in the life of your parish? There is no exact solution to how you may participate, but this exercise may help you get started. Check as many as you wish from the group that follows, or add your own.

Parish Participation Checklist

How I View Participation

___ my responsibility	___ too time consuming
___ part of being Christian	___ a burden
___ an obligation	___ ________________
___ ________________	___ ________________

Remember, ministry does not have to be some eye-popping, soap box performance. It can be whatever you decide to make it, as you choose the best way to live out your baptism along with others in your parish.

Perhaps the photograph that follows may help you explore what you may want to do in your parish. This water scene has an obvious baptismal connection, but look more closely at the lake's reflection of itself. Imagine standing at lakeside, looking directly at the water. What might you see? Indeed, by looking at yourself as in a mirror, you may see where some answers for your questions about ministry lie: in yourself.

The persistence of a Christian may result in solidifying one's belief in Christ, but this persistence may not be built on some unforgettable, miraculous, life-changing event. Yet it may continue after baptism in some gentle, modified way. Note this more complete statement of one newly baptized person (see page 220) in recalling some of her thoughts before baptism:

> I always felt (and not that anybody knew—it wasn't published that I wasn't baptized and it wasn't that all my friends were Catholic)...but I always felt

> that I was missing out on something. You know, I felt that that would make me more whole. I was outgoing but I was insecure... and as I was approaching baptism I felt that that would tie everything together for me... and then I would be this person that would stand up and... this is what I believe in and I'd have a foundation to believe in it.

Another newly baptized person likened her gathering with others to a regular "diabetes injection." She said, "I used to look forward to going down into the rectory every Sunday morning for the catechumenate meetings.... I just had a ball!"

Only you can assess what your journey of faith has been for you and how it may continue. One hint or help, however, may lie in how willing you are to maintain contact with others in your parish. Remaining part of a parish group may not only help in discussing and deciding on a particular way, or ministry, to help out in your parish, but may lead you to explore on an ongoing basis the meaning of your mission for your life of faith.

Did You Know?

The last day of the Easter season is Pentecost Sunday. On this day the Church celebrates the coming and presence of the Holy Spirit among the disciples of Christ. Newly baptized people, like you, may recall praying to the Spirit long before baptism. You also may remember your being confirmed in the Holy Spirit when you were baptized.

Take time now to reflect on the Spirit in your life in the light of two factors:

- the readings from Pentecost Sunday;
- your understanding of your mission as a Christian.

Consider each of the readings now.

The first reading, from the Acts of the Apostles (2:1–11), is the Pentecost account of the coming of the Holy Spirit on Jesus' disciples. The reading states that they were gathered together in one place and "all were filled with the Holy Spirit." The Spirit prompted the disciples to speak of the wonders of God. Today, many Christians believe with great fervor in the nearness and prompting of the Holy Spirit in their lives.

- Are you ever amazed at what you say—as if you had not really planned to state what you expressed? Do you ever sense that God is present in your decisions and actions? Why or why not?

The second reading, from Paul's first letter to the Corinthians (12:3–7, 12–13), includes Paul's classic statement on the many members of the body being one in Christ; Christians are baptized into one body. However, Paul also notes that, "To each person the manifestation of the Spirit is given for the common good." This is a point that may easily be forgotten. The Spirit is not given only for one's own advancement but for the growth of the whole parish community. In other words, a baptized person is not baptized in seclusion, but for the good of others, for Christian discipleship.

- What one decision could you make that might affect the "common good"? Will you make it?

The gospel reading for Pentecost Sunday is from the gospel of John (20:19–23). When you read this gospel passage, you may remember seeing it from the chapter for the second Sunday of Easter. On that day, the passage proclaimed was John 20:19–31.

- In the Pentecost gospel, the risen Christ tells his followers: "As the Father has sent me, so I send you. . . . Receive the Holy Spirit." Do you believe that you are "sent by God" for any particular mission or purpose? What might you do tomorrow to remind yourself of the Spirit of God in your life? Will you do it?

____

____

____

____

ACCEPTING THE CHALLENGE

Your mission for your life of faith—what is it? After seven chapters spanning the entire Easter season, you may have a clarified idea of what it is you are called to be as a baptized person. There is no single answer to determining your mission, though. Each Christian's way of carrying out what he or she believes is linked to what each person is—the broad array of personal, spiritual, social, emotional, and other factors that make you who you are, that make you whole.

Perhaps the photograph you see here can help you to explore one role of the baptized Christian: that of a link, or bridge-builder. Perhaps you have had the opportunity to bring disagreeing people together, if not to reconcile, then at least to talk. On the personal level, such healing and bridge-building is necessary, of course. Indeed, one might wonder if such healing is really an important first step to reducing world tensions. Perhaps a modern day prophet would challenge people and nations to race to embrace rather than race to distrust and potentially destroy.

For a Christian, whether newly baptized or baptized since birth, a key to accepting the challenge of living in Christ may be one's response to the Spirit. Jesus' disciples are not only figures from the past whose names appear in the Bible. Today, Jesus' disciples are Christians who see in the Spirit of God a reality and life that is not just to be read about and studied, but experienced. James McPolin points out that "by communicating his Spirit to disciples, Jesus enables them to continue his own mission which he had received from his Father."[8] A Christian may continue the mission of Jesus within the Church, the community of faith, by praying, celebrating the sacraments, and trusting in the goodness of God, others, and oneself.

- To parallel a question from the first chapter, ask yourself: What could it mean for me now to say that:

  — I hope and trust in myself?

  ____

  ____

  ____

  ____

  — I hope and trust in God?

  ____

  ____

  ____

  ____

  — I hope and trust in others?

  ____

  ____

  ____

  ____

Looking Back

This chapter began with a story of C.M., a woman whose sense of mission took her to South America to work among the poor. Each Christian must work out for him or herself the best way to live one's faith. Whatever way one chooses, one should be mindful of the hope in Christ that joins Christians together. Paul, in his letter to the Romans, says: "For in hope we were saved. Now hope that sees for itself is not hope. For who hopes for what one sees? But if we hope for what we do not see, we wait with endurance" (8:24–25).

As you continue to live as a Christian, you may change some attitudes, see things in a new light, or decide to reconsider decisions you had made that would "never" be changed. Whatever your mission becomes, being patient may help you to discover what makes others think and act as they do when you, perhaps unconsciously, wish they would think and act as you do.

- What might being patient have to do with what you believe your mission is as a Christian?

____

____

____

____

- How can you become more patient in your personal life?

____

____

____

____

Remember your journey to the water of new life and the table of the eucharist. Remember, too, all who have helped you along the way, and all who may be supporting you now. You are one with your parish; you are not alone. Your "going forth to love and serve the Lord" after each Sunday mass may become an example of what it means to live your mission as a Christian community. In the words of St. Augustine:

> Let us sing now, not for the delights of peace, but for the solace of our labor. Just as travelers are accustomed to sing, sing but advance; solace your labor by singing; do not love inactivity; keep singing and keep progressing. What does that mean? Make progress, make progress in well-doing.... If you are progressing, you are advancing; but progress in well-doing, progress in good faith, progress in good deeds. Keep singing and keep advancing.[9]

Now consider one or more of the following:

- Do I really want to stay Christian? Why?

____

____

____

____

- I sometimes wonder about my commitment to my faith because . . .

____

____

____

____

- When things get rough, I turn to ______________________

  because . . . ______________________

  ____

As you conclude, review briefly the sections on exploring the scriptures (pages 221-232) and renewing your life of faith (pages 232-241). Although this is the final review in this book, hopefully it will not be the final review for your life. Try to ask yourself one or two questions each week after your parish's celebration of the eucharist at mass. Perhaps you will want to begin (or continue) a journal of your reflections on your experience as a Christian. Continue to dialogue, to pray, to walk in the newness of life with your parish.

Review now with a sense of clarifying your mission in life and what you can do about it.

- Acts of the Apostles 1:12–14—Prayer is an important part of living as a Christian. Someone I like to pray with is ______________________

  This is because ______________________

  ____

- 1 Peter 4:13–16—I suffer when ______________________

  ____

  ____

- John 17:1–11—When it comes to trying to understand eternal life, I usually think

  ____

  ____

- One way for me to make God's love more obvious in my (home) (job) (parish) (organization) is by ____

____

____

For the section on renewing your life of faith (pages 232-241), select one meaning of eucharist from pages 233-234 and try to apply it to a situation in your own life in a way you ordinarily may not be inclined to do. For example, if you choose to reflect on the eucharist as sacrifice, you may want to decide what sacrifice could mean for you in light of the scripture quote from Isaiah on pages 233-234. If you focus on eucharist as thanksgiving, perhaps you will want to thank God and renew a decision to express thanks to others—when they least expect it.

Now select one word or phrase that best describes you as a person of faith. You may want to recall words used in this book: challenge; new life; center and fullness of faith; way, truth, and life of faith; Jesus; journey; conversion; the Spirit; mission. After you choose your word or phrase, make up one goal for yourself for continuing to live as a Christian. Try to use your word or phrase in your goal statement.

- Goal statement: ____

____

____

____

____

____

____

- Ask yourself: How might I put my goal into practice? Will I do it? __________

____

____

____

____

Conclude this part of your journey with this psalm-prayer (which also appeared in chapter 3) from Psalm 16:8-11:

> I keep the LORD always before me;
>   with the LORD at my right, I shall never be shaken.
> Therefore my heart is glad, my soul rejoices;
>   my body also dwells secure,
> For you will not abandon me to Sheol,
>   nor let your faithful servant see the pit.
> You will show me the path to life,
>   abounding joy in your presence,
>   the delights at your right hand forever.

May your walk in newness of life be ever fresh, ever faithful, and ever joyful! Rejoice and be one with the God who saves and with your beloved sisters and brothers in faith, the Church.

Epilogue

Has it been a challenge for you to pause and reflect on your journey of initiation into the Church? You may have engaged in various events and celebrations, faced interruptions, distractions, and sickness, and even experienced some surprises all during your use of this book. You may have developed some startling new images of what living a life of faith and being a faithful disciple mean for you now. Yet somehow, with the help of the Spirit and support of your parish and its people, you have continued your journey, your pause to enter into the sacred.

Now you may be asking, "Is the Easter season concluded? Do I get back to normal?" But what is normal for you now? Shaped by the gospel, fed at the table of the Lord, your new norm can be enriched by a life of commitment to Jesus and the Church through your community's dynamic celebration of and encounter with Christ in the sacraments. Your pause becomes, then, a movement into a new reality—one that enables you to embrace the light of the Lord Jesus as you grow in discipleship with your parish.

You are called to continue to reflect, to face challenges in your decision-making, to live each day, each moment, as a Christian. It is now time to heighten your resolve to live with an Easter consciousness the rest of your life. Do not be afraid as you renew your life of faith; know that you are not alone, that your parish is with you, that the eyes, ears, hands, feet, and hearts of good and holy people of faith are with you in prayer, in spirit, in trust, in life, in Christ—in all things.

Seek during each month of the next year, on the anniversary of your baptism, and in the years beyond, sustenance from the past as you face the future. Nurture your relationships with others as a people shaped and formed by the word of God in the scriptures. Be part of a eucharistic people, a lively discipleship people in a society that needs your witness and your wisdom.

Yes, there is an Easter season moving toward Pentecost, a crescendo time for celebrating the gift of the Spirit with you, your community, and the whole Church. But as you join in celebration with other neophytes within the supportive embrace of your parish, know that the new life that is yours beckons you forth to the future, to a time beyond that first sharing in Pentecost as one of the faithful.

What can this time beyond Pentecost become? Time is no more than our concrete measure of the divine gift of life, experience, and love of the Creator in our midst. So see beyond the days of a calendar, the digital readout of a watch, the hands of a clock, the sands of an hourglass. Listen to more than the uniform measure of a ticking timepiece; continue to listen to the source of new life—life in Christ—which moves before, after, above, below, through and in time. Become a person not afraid to pause, fearless of journeying beyond time. Gather for and enter into the worship of the Church, and with the whole Church know the limitless love of God.

Continue to journey on the walk of new life with your parish. Leave your timepiece in your drawer and know forever the timeless wonder and endless love of God.

Pause to explore your experience of life, explore the scriptures that sustain your faith, renew the life of faith you call your own, and accept the challenge of discipleship.

Pause to see with fresh eyes of faith your oneness with God and with one another. Pause to seek justice, peace, harmony, and concord.

Because your sacred pause can be more for you than a fleeting moment, make it a new standard for the Christian lifestyle that is yours. In this way, the sacred pause of Easter becomes an Easter consciousness of what you have become and how you live—a pause rich with new directions and perhaps unexpected ventures on the journey of new life.

Notes

INTRODUCTION

1. International Committee on English in the Liturgy (ICEL), *Rite of Christian Initiation of Adults*, no. 244 (Washington, DC: International Committee on English in the Liturgy, 1985); cf. Romans 6:4.

2. Ibid.

3. Gregory Dix, ed., *The Treatise on the Apostolic Tradition of St. Hippolytus of Rome* in H. Chadwick's reissued edition (London: Society for Promoting Christian Knowledge, 1968 [original edition: 1937]), 42.

4. H. Chadwick, trans., *Origen: Contra Celsum* (Cambridge, England: Cambridge University Press, 1965), 165.

5. See Michel Dujarier, *The Rites of Christian Initiation: Historical and Pastoral Reflections*, trans. and ed. by Kevin Hart (New York: William H. Sadlier, Inc., 1979), 209–212 for an excellent summary of these points, with reference to Acts of the Apostles, Justin Martyr, Clement, and Tertullian. Also see E. Evans, trans., *Tertullian's Homily on Baptism* (London: Society for Promoting Christian Knowledge, 1964), 41, 43.

6. For historical information on the length of time of the catechumenate, see W.W. Wilson, trans., *The Writings of Clement of Alexandria* (Edinburgh: T. & T. Clark, 1882), 56–57; and Gregory Dix, ed., *The Treatise on the Apostolic Tradition of St. Hippolytus of Rome* in H. Chadwick's reissued edition (London: Society for Promoting Christian Knowledge, 1968 [original edition: 1937]), 28.

7. One source for this information is Michel Dujarier's *The Rites of Christian Initiation: Historical and Pastoral Reflections*, trans. and ed. by Kevin Hart (New York: William H. Sadlier, Inc., 1979), 91–102. Dujarier cites Egeria, a Spanish nun who had traveled on pilgrimage to Jerusalem, in reporting on the history and meaning of election.

The *RCIA* indicates, in part, the following about the meaning of election for the Church today: "This step is called election because the acceptance made by the Church is founded on the election by God, in whose name the Church acts. The step is also called the enrollment of names because as a pledge of fidelity the candidates inscribe their names in the book that lists those who have been chosen for initiation" (International Committee on English in the Liturgy, *Rite of Christian Initiation of Adults*, no. 119, Washington, DC: International Committee on English in the Liturgy, 1985).

8. Michel Dujarier, *A History of the Catechumenate: The First Six Centuries*, trans. and ed. by Kevin Hart (New York: William H. Sadlier, Inc., 1979), 101–102.

9. For a discussion of the events of Easter week, see Michel Dujarier, *The Rites of Christian Initiation: Historical and Pastoral Reflections*, trans. and ed. by Kevin Hart (New York: William H. Sadlier, Inc., 1979), 208, 212–216. This emphasis on Easter Week is not to deny, of course, the power and formative dimensions of prebaptismal preaching. Some selections, for example, from John Chrysostom in this book are from the days before baptism, and provide a rich resource for pursuing the contemporary postbaptismal experience.

There also existed an element of secrecy in passing on the beliefs and mysteries of the faith. See Edward Yarnold, *The Awe-Inspiring Rites of Initiation* (Slough, England: St. Paul Publications, 1971), 11–12 and 50–54 for background and related discussion of such secrecy.

10. See Hugh M. Riley, *Christian Initiation: A Comparative Study of the Interpretation of the Baptismal Liturgy in the Mystagogical Writings of Cyril of Jerusalem, John Chrysostom, Theodore of Mopsuestia, and Ambrose of Milan* (Washington, DC: The Catholic University of America Press, 1974), especially 1–10 and Michel Dujarier, *The Rites of Christian Initiation: Historical and Pastoral Reflections*, trans. and ed. by Kevin Hart (New York: William H. Sadlier, Inc., 1979), 214–215. For a concise and insightful analysis of particular aspects of the era with application to contemporary practice see Catherine Dooley, "Liturgical Catechesis: Mystagogy, Marriage or Misnomer?" *Worship* 66, no. 5 (September 1992): 386–397.

11. Edward Yarnold, *The Awe-Inspiring Rites of Initiation* (Slough, England: St. Paul Publications, 1971), 54.

12. The interested reader may choose to pursue study of these fathers in Hugh M. Riley, *Christian Initiation: A Comparative Study of the Interpretation of the Baptismal Liturgy in the Mystagogical Writings of Cyril of Jerusalem, John Chrysostom, Theodore of Mopsuestia, and Ambrose of Milan* (Washington, DC: The Catholic University of

America Press, 1974) and Enrico Mazza, *Mystagogy: A Theology of Liturgy in the Patristic Age*, trans. Matthew J. O'Connell (New York: Pueblo Publishing Company, 1989).

Some evidence suggests that the mystagogical catecheses credited to Cyril should instead be identified as those of John of Jerusalem, Cyril's successor as bishop.

13. See Note 10.

14. National Conference of Catholic Bishops, "A Glossary of Terms for Initiation," *Bishops' Committee on the Liturgy Newsletter* 14 (October 1978): 134.

15. ICEL, *RCIA*, no. 247.

16. Scripture verses in this section are taken from the New American Bible *Lectionary for Mass* (New York: Catholic Book Publishing Co., 1970).

17. ICEL, *RCIA*, no. 246.

18. National Conference of Catholic Bishops, *Communities of Salt and Light: Reflections on the Social Mission of the Parish* (Washington, DC: United States Catholic Conference, Inc., 1994), 12.

CHAPTER 1

1. Anthony A. Stephenson, trans., "Procatechesis 16, 17," in *The Works of Saint Cyril of Jerusalem*, vol. 1, trans. Leo P. McCauley and Anthony A. Stephenson (Washington, DC: The Catholic University of America Press, 1969), 82–84.

2. Anthony A. Stephenson, trans., "First Lecture on the Mysteries, 4–8," in *The Works of Saint Cyril of Jerusalem*, vol. 2, trans. Leo P. McCauley and Anthony A. Stephenson (Washington, DC: The Catholic University of America Press, 1970), 155–157.

3. Roy J. Deferrari, trans., "The Mysteries, 2:5," *Saint Ambrose: Theological and Dogmatic Works* (Washington, DC: The Catholic University of America Press, 1963), 6.

4. Leo P. McCauley, trans., "Catechesis 5:4," in *The Works of Saint Cyril of Jerusalem*, vol. 1, trans. Leo P. McCauley and Anthony A. Stephenson (Washington, DC: The Catholic University of America Press, 1969), 141.

5. Leo P. McCauley, trans., "Catechesis 5:12," in *The Works of Saint Cyril of Jerusalem*, vol. 1, trans. Leo P. McCauley and Anthony A. Stephenson (Washington, DC: The Catholic University of America Press, 1970), 146.

6. Anthony A. Stephenson, trans., "First Lecture on the Mysteries, 9," in *The Works of Saint Cyril of Jerusalem*, vol. 2, trans. Leo P. McCauley and Anthony A. Stephenson (Washington, DC: The Catholic University of America Press, 1970), 158–159.

7. International Committee on English in the Liturgy, *Rite of Christian Initiation of Adults*, no. 233 (Washington, DC: International Committee on English in the Liturgy, 1985).

8. Anthony A. Stephenson, trans., "Second Lecture on the Mysteries, 8," in *The Works of Saint Cyril of Jerusalem*, vol. 2, trans. Leo P. McCauley and Anthony A. Stephenson (Washington, DC: The Catholic University of America Press, 1970), 167.

CHAPTER 2

1. Editorial: "Heed Official Advice," *Wilkes-Barre Times Leader, The Evening News, Wilkes-Barre Record*, 29 June 1972.

2. Thomas E. Durkish, *Priory Poems* (Chestertown, NY: Booklet available from Priory of St. Benedict, 1978).

3. International Committee on English in the Liturgy (ICEL), *Rite of Christian Initiation of Adults*, no. 210 (Washington, DC: International Committee on English in the Liturgy, 1985).

4. ICEL, *RCIA*, no. 222.

5. ICEL, *RCIA*, no. 226.

6. ICEL, *RCIA*, no. 215.

7. For a thorough exploration of this topic, see Hugh M. Riley, *Christian Initiation: A Comparative Study of the Interpretation of the Baptismal Liturgy in the Mystagogical Writings of Cyril of Jerusalem, John Chrysostom, Theodore of Mopsuestia, and Ambrose of Milan* (Washington, DC: The Catholic University of America Press, 1974).

8. A. Mingana, ed. and trans., "Theodore on Baptism, Chapter IV," *Commentary of Theodore of Mopsuestia on the Lord's Prayer and on the Sacraments of Baptism and the Eucharist* (Cambridge, England: W. Heffer & Sons, Limited, 1933), 54–55; delivered prior to baptism.

9. Paul W. Harkins, trans., "Baptismal Instruction, 2:25, 26," *St. John Chrysostom: Baptismal Instructions* (New York: Newman Press, 1963), 52-53. Harkins notes that this instruction preceded the baptismal event. See his note 1 on page 213.

10. Paul W. Harkins, trans., "Baptismal Instruction, 2, 29," *St. John Chrysostom: Baptismal Instructions* (New York: Newman Press, 1963), 54. Harkins notes that this instruction preceded the baptismal event. See his note 1 on page 213.

11. Paul W. Harkins, trans., "Baptismal Instruction 7:25, 27," *St. John Chrysostom: Baptismal Instructions* (New York: Newman Press, 1963), 114–115.

12. Elaine Holena-Baumbach, "Baptism," Unpublished poem, 1978.

13. ICEL, *RCIA*, no. 230.

CHAPTER 3

1. International Committee on English in the Liturgy (ICEL), *Rite of Christian Initiation of Adults*, no. 243 (Washington, DC: International Committee on English in the Liturgy, 1985).

2. Roy J. Deferrari, trans., "The Sacraments 4:5; 5:14," *Saint Ambrose: Theological and Dogmatic Works* (Washington, DC: The Catholic University of America Press, 1963), 298–299, 300, 313.

3. Ralph A. Keifer, *Blessed and Broken: An Explanation of the Contemporary Experience of God in Eucharistic Celebration* (Wilmington, DE: Michael Glazier, Inc., 1982), 70–71.

4. ICEL, *RCIA*, no. 217.

5. Walt Whitman, "Song of the Open Road" from *Leaves of Grass* in Mark van Doren, *Walt Whitman: The Viking Portable Library* (New York: The Viking Press, 1945 [revised in 1973 by Malcolm Cowley]), 166–167.

6. Roy J. Deferrari, trans., "The Mysteries, 1:3," *Saint Ambrose: Theological and Dogmatic Works* (Washington, DC: The Catholic University of America Press, 1963), 6.

7. National Conference of Catholic Bishops, *The Harvest of Justice Is Sown in Peace: A Reflection of the National Conference of Bishops on the Tenth Anniversary of* The Challenge of Peace (Washington, DC: United States Catholic Conference, 1994), 10.

8. Stephen T. DeMott, Editorial: "Give Them Something to Eat," *Maryknoll*, July/August 1994, 7.

9. Thomas Merton, *The Silent Life* (New York: Farrar, Straus, & Giroux, 1975), vii.

10. ICEL, *RCIA*, no. 243.

11. Gregory Dix, ed., *The Treatise on the Apostolic Tradition of St. Hippolytus of Rome* in H. Chadwick's reissued edition (London: Society for Promoting Christian Knowledge, 1968 [original edition: 1937]), 42.

12. Roy J. Deferrari, trans., "The Mysteries, 8:46," *Saint Ambrose: Theological and Dogmatic Works* (Washington, DC: The Catholic University of America Press, 1963), 22.

13. John H. Westerhoff, *Building God's People in a Materialistic Society* (New York: Seabury, 1983), 89.

CHAPTER 4

1. International Committee on English in the Liturgy (ICEL), *Rite of Christian Initiation of Adults*, no. 220 (Washington, DC: International Committee on English in the Liturgy, 1985).

2. Paul W. Harkins, trans., "Baptismal Instruction, 5:20," *St. John Chrysostom: Baptismal Instructions* (New York: Newman Press, 1963), 88–89.

3. National Conference of Catholic Bishops, *The Harvest of Justice Is Sown in Peace: A Reflection of the National Conference of Bishops on the Tenth Anniversary of* The Challenge of Peace (Washington, DC: United States Catholic Conference, 1994), 2.

4. Roy J. Deferrari, trans., "The Sacraments, 3:15," *Saint Ambrose: Theological and Dogmatic Works* (Washington, DC: The Catholic University of America Press, 1963), 295.

5. Thomas E. Durkish, *Priory Poems* (Chestertown, NY: Booklet available from Priory of St. Benedict, 1978).

6. ICEL, *RCIA*, no. 222.

7. Paul W. Harkins, trans., "Baptismal Instruction, 4:1, 2," *St. John Chrysostom: Baptismal Instructions* (New York: Newman Press, 1963), 66.

8. ICEL, *RCIA*, no. 246.

9. Anthony A. Stephenson, trans., "Second Lecture on the Mysteries, 4, 5," in *The Works of Saint Cyril of Jerusalem*, vol. 2, trans. Leo P. McCauley and Anthony A. Stephenson (Washington, DC: The Catholic University of America Press, 1970), 163–165.

CHAPTER 5

1. William Barclay, *The Gospel of John*, vol. 2, rev. ed. (Philadelphia: The Westminster Press, 1975), 152.

2. International Committee on English in the Liturgy (ICEL), *Rite of Christian Initiation of Adults*, no. 244 (Washington, DC: International Committee on English in the Liturgy, 1985).

3. Edward Yarnold, trans., "Theodore of Mopsuestia—Baptismal Homily 4:9," in his *The Awe-Inspiring Rites of Initiation* (Slough, England: St. Paul Publications, 1971), 215.

4. International Committee on English in the Liturgy (ICEL), *The Roman Missal: The Sacramentary* (Washington, DC: International Committee on English in the Liturgy, 1973), 206.

5. Ibid., 415.

6. Anthony A. Stephenson, trans., "Fifth Lecture on the Mysteries, 4," in *The Works of Saint Cyril of Jerusalem*, vol. 2, trans. Leo P. McCauley and Anthony A. Stephenson (Washington, DC: The Catholic University of America Press, 1970), 193–194.

7. ICEL, *The Roman Missal: The Sacramentary*, 415.

8. Edward Yarnold, trans., "Theodore of Mopsuestia—Baptismal Homily 4:4, 5," in his *The Awe-Inspiring Rites of Initiation* (Slough, England: St. Paul Publications, 1971), 213.

9. Anthony A. Stephenson, trans., "Fifth Lecture on the Mysteries, 3," in *The Works of Saint Cyril of Jerusalem*, vol. 2, trans. Leo P. McCauley and Anthony A. Stephenson (Washington, DC: The Catholic University of America Press, 1970), 192–193.

10. Roy J. Deferrari, trans., "The Mysteries 9:54," *Saint Ambrose: Theological and Dogmatic Works* (Washington, DC: The Catholic University of America Press, 1963), 26.

CHAPTER 6

1. Paul W. Harkins, trans., "Baptismal Instruction, 11:16," *St. John Chrysostom: Baptismal Instructions* (New York: Newman Press, 1963), 165. Harkins identifies this instruction as the last one delivered to those seeking baptism, two days before the sacramental celebration, that is, on Holy Thursday. See his note 2 on page 314.

2. Paul W. Harkins, trans., "Baptismal Instruction, 11:32, 33," *St. John Chrysostom: Baptismal Instructions* (New York: Newman Press, 1963), 171. Harkins identifies this instruction as the last one delivered to those seeking baptism, two days before the sacramental celebration, that is, on Holy Thursday. See his note 2 on page 314.

3. Anthony A. Stephenson, trans., "Fifth Lecture on the Mysteries, 7," in *The Works of Saint Cyril of Jerusalem*, vol. 2, trans. Leo P. McCauley and Anthony A. Stephenson (Washington, DC: The Catholic University of America Press, 1970), 196.

4. Gerard F. Baumbach, Diary entry, January 10, 1980.

5. Thomas Marsh, *Gift of Community: Baptism and Confirmation* (Wilmington, DE: Michael Glazier, Inc., 1984), 157.

6. International Committee on English in the Liturgy (ICEL), *Rite of Christian Initiation of Adults*, no. 234 (Washington, DC: International Committee on English in the Liturgy, 1985).

7. ICEL, *RCIA*, no. 235.

8. Anthony A. Stephenson, trans., "Third Lecture on the Mysteries, 2," in *The Works of Saint Cyril of Jerusalem*, vol. 2, trans. Leo P. McCauley and Anthony A. Stephenson (Washington, DC: The Catholic University of America Press, 1970), 170.

9. Anthony A. Stephenson, trans., "Fourth Lecture on the Mysteries, 6," in *The Works of Saint Cyril of Jerusalem*, vol. 2, trans. Leo P. McCauley and Anthony A. Stephenson (Washington, DC: The Catholic University of America Press, 1970), 183.

10. International Committee on English in the Liturgy (ICEL), *The Roman Missal: The Sacramentary* (Washington, DC: International Committee on English in the Liturgy, 1973), 549.

11. ICEL, *The Roman Missal: The Sacramentary*, 549.

12. ICEL, *The Roman Missal: The Sacramentary*, 550.

13. Roy J. Deferrari, trans., "The Sacraments, 4:16," *Saint Ambrose: Theological and Dogmatic Works* (Washington, DC: The Catholic University of America Press, 1963), 302–303.

14. ICEL, *The Roman Missal: The Sacramentary*, 550.

15. ICEL, *The Roman Missal: The Sacramentary*, 551.

16. W. A. Jurgens, trans., "Sermon 272," *The Faith of the Early Fathers*, vol. 3 (Collegeville, MN: The Liturgical Press, 1979), 32.

17. Anthony A. Stephenson, trans., "Fifth Lecture on the Mysteries, 21, 22," in *The Works of Saint Cyril of Jerusalem*, vol. 2, trans. Leo P. McCauley and Anthony A. Stephenson (Washington, DC: The Catholic University of America Press, 1970), 203.

18. A. Mingana, ed. and trans., "Theodore on Eucharist and Liturgy, Chapter VI," *Commentary of Theodore of Mopsuestia on the Lord's Prayer and on the Sacraments of Baptism and the Eucharist* (Cambridge, England: W. Heffer & Sons, Limited, 1933), 104.

19. Anthony A. Stephenson, trans., "Fifth Lecture on the Mysteries, 23," in *The Works of Saint Cyril of Jerusalem*, vol. 2, trans. Leo P. McCauley and Anthony A. Stephenson (Washington, DC: The Catholic University of America Press, 1970), 203.

CHAPTER 7

1. C. M., letter to author dated January 11, 1986.

2. Ibid., July, 1986.

3. Ibid., December, 1986.

4. United States Catholic Conference, *Putting Children and Families First: A Challenge for Our Church, Nation, and World* (Washington, DC: United States Catholic Conference, Inc., 1992), 1.

5. International Committee on English in the Liturgy, *The Roman Missal: The Sacramentary* (Washington, DC: International Committee on English in the Liturgy, 1973), 565, 567.

6. A. Mingana, ed. and trans., "Theodore on Eucharist and Liturgy, Chapter VI," *Commentary of Theodore of Mopsuestia on the Lord's Prayer and on the Sacraments of Baptism and the Eucharist* (Cambridge, England: W. Heffer & Sons, Limited, 1933), 114.

7. Ibid., 115–116.

8. James McPolin, *John* (Wilmington, DE: Michael Glazier, Inc., 1979), 257.

9. M. Sarah Muldowney, trans., "Sermon 256," *Saint Augustine: Sermons on the Liturgical Seasons* (New York: Fathers of the Church, Inc., 1959), 362.